JEAN MOSS

DESIGNER KNITS COLLECTION

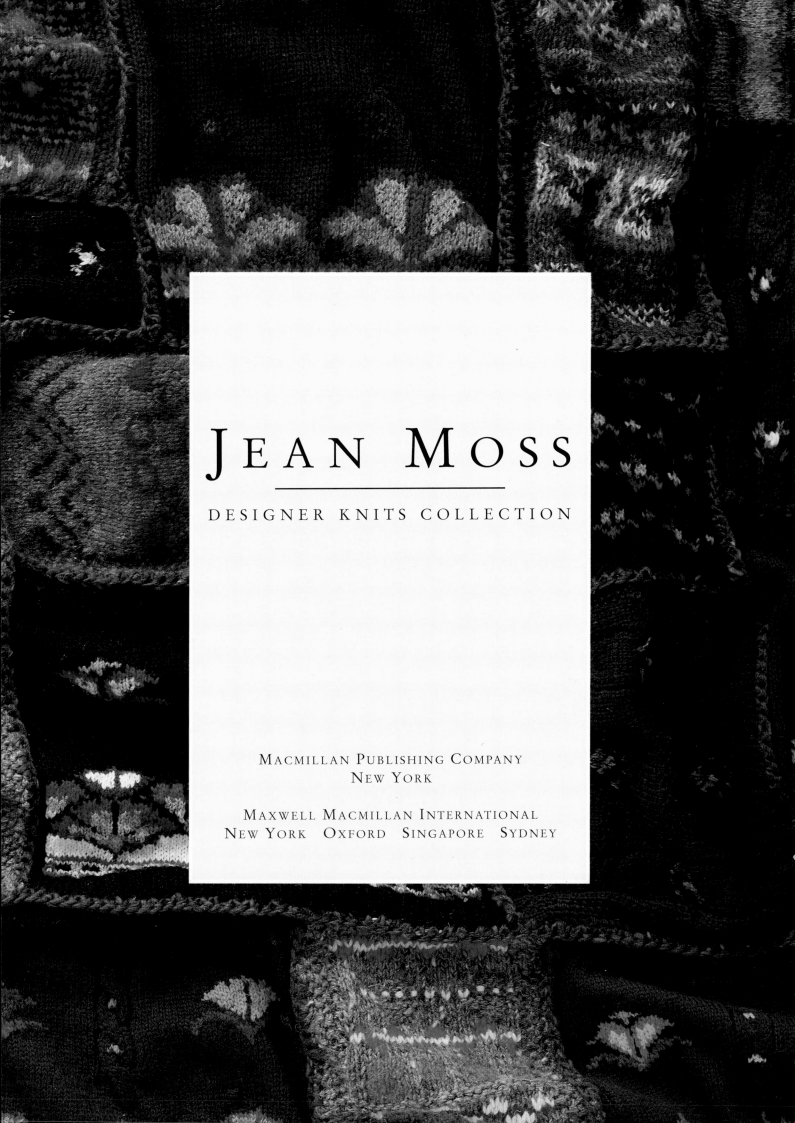

JEAN MOSS

DESIGNER KNITS COLLECTION

MACMILLAN PUBLISHING COMPANY
NEW YORK

MAXWELL MACMILLAN INTERNATIONAL
NEW YORK   OXFORD   SINGAPORE   SYDNEY

To BRIAN FOR HIS LOVE AND ENCOURAGEMENT

Macmillan Publishing Company
866 Third Avenue
New York, NY 10022

Macmillan Publishing Company is part of the Maxwell
Communication Group of Companies.

Library of Congress Cataloging-in-Publication Data
Moss, Jean
Jean Moss designer knits collection
p.   cm.
ISBN 0-02-587555-8
1. Knitting-Patterns.   2. Sweaters.   I. Title
TT825.M68   1991   746.9'2-dc20   91-10853 CIP

Macmillan books are available at special discounts for
bulk purchases for sales promotions, premiums, fund-
raising, or educational use. For details, contact:
Special Sales Director
Macmillan Publishing Company
866 Third Avenue
New York, NY 10022

10 9 8 7 6 5 4 3 2 1

Printed in Hong Kong

4

CONTENTS

*Sweaters marked with an asterisk are
available as kits—see page 160

INTRODUCTION

I will always remember being taught to knit as a child by my grandmother in Lancashire. Although I could not have been more than three years old, I can still recall with pleasure how delighted I was to be able to create something of interest and value out of lengths of yarn.

Another invaluable childhood lesson was that I should take care to really look at the things around me – to try to experience them with all my senses. For this lesson I am eternally grateful to my early teachers; for it was a wonderful gift. It gave me a deep curiosity about the past – the traditions, customs and relics from other cultures and times. Through my knitting I have been able to indulge this passion and express it artistically.

My professional knitting began about fifteen years ago when my late husband, Brian, and I and our two young children were living in an old Georgian farmhouse, deep in the Yorkshire Wolds. To get to our farmhouse we had to go down a long dirt track through four fields with gates and motley farm animals.

Living in such an isolated place we had difficulty at first finding paid work without travelling long distances. Before the children started school we were able to make ends meet by playing guitar and singing our own songs in folk clubs around Britain. But once the children started school our travels were restricted and we had to rethink things.

After trying everything from setting up a wholefood shop to painting and decorating, we finally hit on the idea of my buying a knitting machine and trying to design some sweaters. Necessity had dictated that I made most of my own clothes anyway, and friends were always asking me to make things for them, so we decided to try to produce sweaters commercially.

A friend of a friend happened to have a boutique in Camden Town, London; and her shop, *du du*, took all of the sweaters we made for the first two or three years of our venture. Eventually we expanded the business, employing some local machine knitters. I started to show my collections at exhibitions in London, and on one such occasion I was asked by Ralph Lauren's agent if I might be interested in designing some handknits for him. This inspired me to go back to my original roots and start working on handknits again.

Free from the restrictions of the machine I became very excited by the whole new world of possibilities that handknits opened up and I gave my imagination full rein. I began studying as many old knitting patterns as I could get my hands on, discovering a wealth of skill and creativity in them.

My search for interesting sources also

Photograph: Philip Mercer

led me into other decorative arts of the past. For their beautiful use of colour and incredible technical skill I had always loved antique textiles from all over the world, from samplers and embroideries to tapestries and oriental carpets. These were joined by other sources such as stained glass, medieval illuminated manuscripts, old china, as well as the more modern pottery of the Art Deco movement, American Indian and African beadwork, sculptures and carvings – in fact anything which could be interpreted in my knitting was hungrily devoured. I would go out on trips with my camera, making a pictorial note of the wonderful colours, textures and forms that both nature and human beings have created.

While working with Ralph Lauren on many of his collections, I learned so much about styling and shaping sweaters. I became more aware of the large part that the fit of a sweater has to play if it is to be a joy to wear, and found that this must surely be one of the keys to creating elegant and beautiful knitwear. Since then I have gone on to work with many other design houses, such as Calvin Klein, Laura Ashley, Benetton, as well as to design my own handknit collections twice a year.

To me an old knitted sweater has a multitude of meanings. It reminds me of the woman who knitted it, her life, and the lives of her family and community. I try in my design work to retain the traditional beauty, skill and craftsmanship, interpreting old sweaters in new ways, but essentially retaining the integrity of the source which inspired it.

Each of my sweater designs has been created with a love and respect for the traditions and cultures of the past – the crusty old cables and Arans of the crofters and fisher folk, the incredible celebration of colour and technique of the Fair Isles, the intricacy of antique lacework, as well as the practical, hard-wearing qualities which were once such a necessity.

I believe that there is no sweater without a wearer, and with this always in mind, I try to create sweaters in which people will feel comfortable, which are beautiful in their own right, but which, when worn, will allow the wearer to make her or his own statement, always to complement and never to dominate their personality.

There are many hours of knitting in this book, and I hope that you will see each sweater that you choose to knit as a special journey through the wonderful legacies of the past. I have always wished to design sweaters which will transcend fashion, which are timeless, and I hope that the ones in this book will become just as much your old favourites as they are mine.

Jean Moss

COUNTRY GARDEN

WITH LEISURELY WALKS IN COUNTRY

GARDENS IN MIND I TOOK MY INSPIRATION

FOR THE EIGHT SWEATERS IN THIS SECTION

FROM A WIDE RANGE OF TRADITIONAL

SOURCES INCLUDING THE BOLD COLOUR OF

THE POTTERY OF CLARICE CLIFF AND THE

CLASSIC TEXTURES OF ARAN SWEATERS.

MAKING SOMETHING NEW AND UNUSUAL

FROM SOMETHING WHICH IS OLD AND

FAMILIAR IS A CHALLENGE I LOVE TO

TAKE UP IN MY DESIGN WORK.

SISSINGHURST

HERE IS ONE OF MY FAVOURITE SWEATERS — UNDERSTATED

SCULPTURED LOVEBIRDS NESTLE BETWEEN THE DELICATE SPRING

FLOWERS, EACH CAMEO FRAMED BY SMALL CABLES.

◆

MATERIALS
600g/21¼oz of a lightweight mercerised cotton in main colour A
50g/1¾oz each of contrast colours B, C, D, E, F and G
Pair each of 2¼mm (US 1) and 3mm (US 3) knitting needles
Extra pair of 2¼mm (US 1) knitting needles
Cable needle

MEASUREMENTS
Actual measurements
Bust 95cm/37½in
Length to shoulders 63.5cm/25in
Sleeve seam 52.5cm/20¾in

TENSION/GAUGE
38 sts and 40 rows to 10cm/4in measured over patt worked on 3mm (US 3) needles

Please check your tension/gauge carefully and change needle size if necessary

NOTE
When working from chart use separate small balls of yarn for each isolated area of colour and twist yarns together at WS of work when changing colour to avoid making a hole.

BACK
Using smaller needles and A cast on 161 sts.
Rib row 1 (RS) K1, * p1, k1, rep from * to end of row.

Rib row 2 P1, * k1, p1, rep from * to end.
Rep these 2 rows for 6.5cm/2½in ending with rib row 1.
Inc row Rib 9, * M1, rib 8, rep from * to end. 180 sts.
Change to larger needles.
Work in patt from chart as follows:
Row 1 (RS) Work last 18 sts of row 1, then work 72 st patt rep twice, then work first 18 sts of row 1.
Row 2 Work last 18 sts of row 2, then work 72 st patt rep twice, then work first 18 sts of row 2.
Cont straight in patt until back measures approximately 39cm/15½in from cast-on edge, ending with row 2.
Shape armholes
Cast/bind off 8 sts at beg of next 2 rows. 164 sts.
Cont straight in patt until back measures 63.5cm/25in from cast-on edge, ending with a WS row.
Shape shoulders
Cast/bind off 53 sts at beg of next 2 rows.
Leave rem 58 sts on a spare needle.

FRONT
Work as given for back until front measures 45.5cm/18in from beg ending with a WS row.
Shape neck
Next row Patt 82 sts, turn and leave rem sts on a spare needle.

** Dec 1 st at neck edge of next and every foll alt row until 53 sts rem.

Cont straight until front measures the same as back to shoulder ending at armhole edge.

Shape shoulder

Cast/bind off 53 sts. ******

With right side facing, join yarn to rem sts and patt to end.

Complete to match first side from ****** to ******.

SLEEVES

Using smaller needles and A cast on 65 sts.

Work 8cm/3in rib as given for back, ending with a RS row.

Inc row Rib 2, M1, rib 3, * M1, rib 2, M1, rib 3, rep from * to end. 90 sts.

Change to larger needles.

Work in patt from chart as follow:

Row 1 (RS) Work last 9 sts of row 1, then work 72 st patt rep once, then work first 9 sts of row 1.

Row 2 Work last 9 sts of row 2, then work 72 st patt rep once, then work first 9 sts of row 2.

Inc and work into patt 1 st each end of the next and every foll 4th row until there are 180 sts.

Cont straight until sleeve measures 54.5cm/ 21½in from cast-on edge, ending with a WS row.

Cast/bind off.

COLLAR

Join shoulder seams.

With right side facing, using smaller needles and A pick up and k 70 sts up right side of front neck, on to another needle k across 58 sts on back neck, on to a 3rd needle pick up and k 70 sts down left side of front neck. 198 sts. Turning at centre front, work rib in rows as follows:

Row 1 * P1, k1, rep from * to end.

Row 2 * K1, p1, rep from * to end.

Rep these 2 rows for 5cm/2in.

Cast/bind off.

FINISHING

Set in sleeves, sewing last 8 rows to 8 sts cast/ bound off at underarm. Join side and sleeve seams.

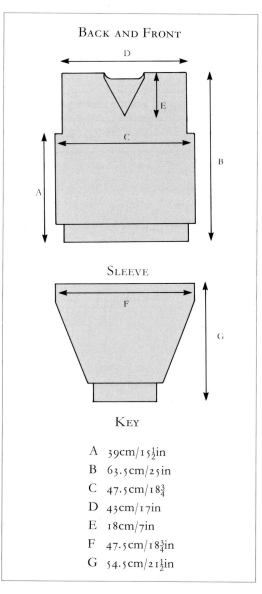

BACK AND FRONT

SLEEVE

KEY

A 39cm/15½in

B 63.5cm/25in

C 47.5cm/18¾

D 43cm/17in

E 18cm/7in

F 47.5cm/18¾in

G 54.5cm/21½in

PATTERN CHART

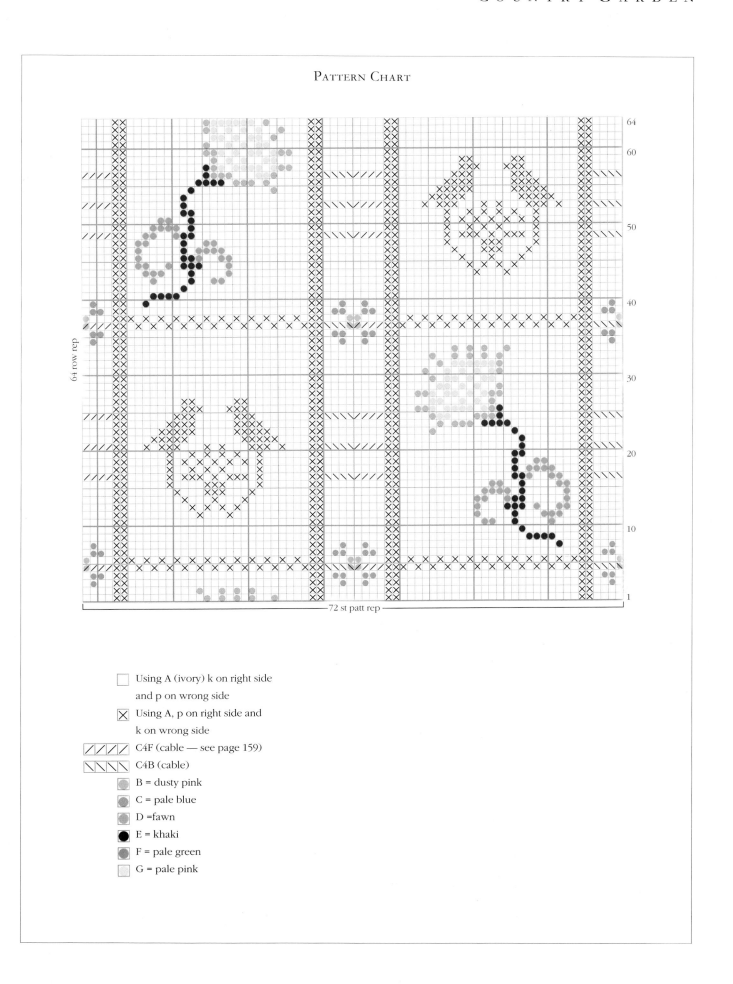

Using A (ivory) k on right side
and p on wrong side

Using A, p on right side and
k on wrong side

C4F (cable — see page 159)

C4B (cable)

B = dusty pink

C = pale blue

D = fawn

E = khaki

F = pale green

G = pale pink

VERSAILLES

CREATED WITH SUMMER GARDEN PARTIES IN MIND, THIS

ELEGANT JACKET IS MY ATTEMPT TO CAPTURE THE FRAGILE

ESSENCE OF EARLY SPRING FLOWERS AND THE DELICATE

SUBTLETY OF THEIR COLOURS.

———————◆———————

MATERIALS
450g/16oz of a lightweight mercerised cotton in main colour A
50g/1¾oz each of contrast colours B and C
25g/1oz each of contrast colours D, E, F, G, H and I
Pair each of 2¼mm (US 1) and 3¼mm (US 3) knitting needles
7 buttons

MEASUREMENTS
Actual measurements
Bust 95cm/37½in
Length to shoulders 53cm/21in
Sleeve seam 45cm/17¾in

TENSION/GAUGE
30 sts and 38 rows to 10cm/4in measured over st st worked on 3¼mm (US 3) needles

Please check your tension/gauge carefully and change needle size if necessary

NOTE
When working from charts use separate small balls of yarn for each isolated area of colour and twist yarns together at WS of work when changing colour to avoid making a hole.

BACK
Using smaller needles and A cast on 198 sts.
K 2 rows.
Change to larger needles and work from peplum chart B in patt as follows:

Row 1 (RS) K14, * [p1, k1] 7 times, p1, k16, rep from * 4 times more, [p1, k1] 7 times, p1, k14.
Row 2 P15, * [k1, p1] 6 times, k1, p18, rep from * 4 times more, [k1, p1] 6 times, k1, p15.
Rows 3 and 4 As rows 1 and 2.
Work from chart shaping as follows:
Row 5 K12, * sl 1, k1, psso, k2, [p1, k1] 5 times, p1, k2, k2 tog, k12, rep from * to end.
Row 6 P14, * [k1, p1] 6 times, k1, p16, rep from * 4 times more, [k1, p1] 6 times, k1, p14.
Row 7 K15, * [p1, k1] 5 times, p1, k18, rep from * 4 times more, [p1, k1] 5 times, p1, k15.
Row 8 P14, * [k1, p1] 6 times, k1, p16, rep from * 4 times more, [k1, p1] 6 times, k1, p14.
Row 9 K12, * sl 1, k1, psso, k1, [p1, k1] 6 times, k2 tog, k12, rep from * to end.
Row 10 P15, * [k1, p1] 4 times, k1, p18, rep from * 4 times more, [k1, p1] 4 times, k1, p15.
Row 11 K14, * [p1, k1] 5 times, p1, k16, rep from * 4 times more, [p1, k1] 5 times, p1, k14.
Row 12 P15, * [k1, p1] 4 times, k1, p18, rep from * 4 times more, [k1, p1] 4 times, k1, p15.
Row 13 K12, * sl 1, k1, psso, k2, [p1, k1] 3 times, p1, k2, k2 tog, k12, rep from * to end.
Cont in this way decreasing 1 st each side of every foll 4th row until 32 rows have been

worked and 114 sts rem.

Now work from back chart C, increasing 1 st each end of the 16th and every foll 4th row until there are 142 sts then work straight until row 84 has been worked.

Shape armholes

Cast/bind off 9 sts at beg of next 2 rows.

Dec 1 st at each end of the next 2 rows and 3 foll alt rows. 114 sts.

Cont to end of chart working neck and shoulder shaping as shown.

LEFT FRONT

Using smaller needles and A cast on 97 sts. K2 rows.

Change to larger needles and work from peplum chart A as follows:

Row 1 (RS) K10, * [p1, k1] 7 times, p1, k16, rep from * once more, [p1, k1] 7 times, p1, k10.

Row 2 P11, * [k1, p1] 6 times, k1, p18, rep from * once more, [k1, p1] 6 times, k1, p11.

Rows 3 and 4 As rows 1 and 2.

Row 5 K8, * sl 1, k1, psso, k2, [p1, k1] 5 times, p1, k2, k2 tog, k12, rep from * ending last rep k8.

Row 6 P10, * [k1, p1] 6 times, k1, p16, rep from * ending last rep p10.

Row 7 K11, * [p1, k1] 5 times, p1, k18, rep from * ending last rep k11.

Row 8 P10, * [k1, p1] 6 times, k1, p16, rep from * ending last rep p10.

Row 9 K8, * sl 1, k1, psso, k1, [p1, k1] 6 times, k2 tog, k12, rep from * ending last rep k8.

Cont in this way decreasing 1 st each side of

every foll 4th row until 32 rows have been worked and 55 sts rem.

Now work from left front chart D, increasing 1 st at end of the 16th and every foll 4th row until there are 69 sts then work straight until row 84 has been worked.

Shape armhole

Cast/bind off 9 sts at beg of next row.

Dec 1 st at armhole edge of the next 2 rows and 3 foll alt rows. 55 sts.

Work straight to end of row 103.

Shape neck

Cont to end of chart working neck and shoulder shaping as shown.

RIGHT FRONT

Work as given for left front reversing all shapings and foll peplum chart A and right front chart E.

SLEEVES

Using smaller needles and A cast on 64 sts. Work 10cm/4in k1, p1 rib, ending with a RS row.

Inc row Rib 4, * M1, rib 5, rep from * to end. 76 sts.

Change to larger needles and work from chart, shaping sides of sleeves as shown, until row 187 has been worked. 56 sts rem.

Row 188 K1, * k3 tog, rep from * to last st, k1.

Cast/bind off.

FRONT BAND

Using smaller needles and A cast on 9 sts and beg patt as follows:

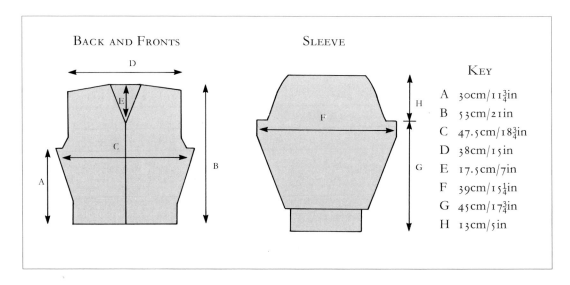

BACK AND FRONTS

SLEEVE

KEY

A 30cm/11¾in

B 53cm/21in

C 47.5cm/18¾in

D 38cm/15in

E 17.5cm/7in

F 39cm/15¼in

G 45cm/17¾in

H 13cm/5in

Patt row K1, * p1, k1, rep from * to end.
This row forms the patt and is repeated throughout.
Work 3 rows in patt.
Buttonhole row 1 Patt 4, cast/bind off 2 sts, patt to end.
Buttonhole row 2 Patt to end, casting on 2 sts over those cast/bound off in previous row.

Cont in patt, working 6 more buttonholes 5 cm/2in above cast/bound off edge of previous buttonhole.

Cont in patt until band, when slightly stretched, fits up right front around back neck and down left front.

FINISHING

Join shoulder seams. Sew on front band with the 7th buttonhole level with the first row of neck shaping on the right front. Set in sleeves. Join side and sleeve seams. Sew on buttons.

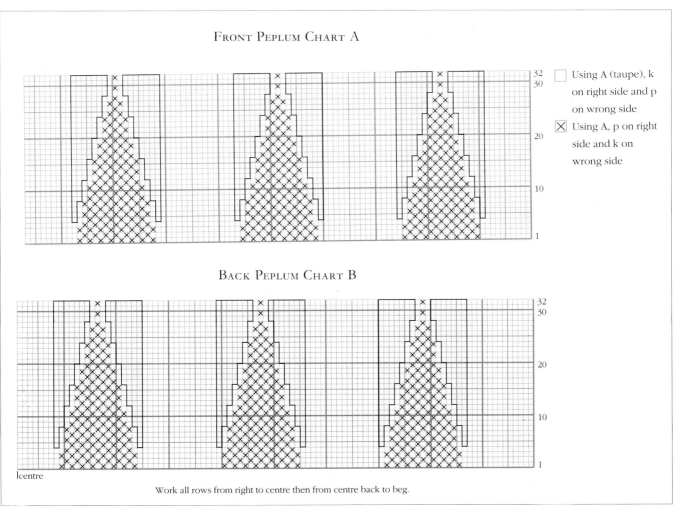

FRONT PEPLUM CHART A

☐ Using A (taupe), k on right side and p on wrong side

☒ Using A, p on right side and k on wrong side

BACK PEPLUM CHART B

|centre

Work all rows from right to centre then from centre back to beg.

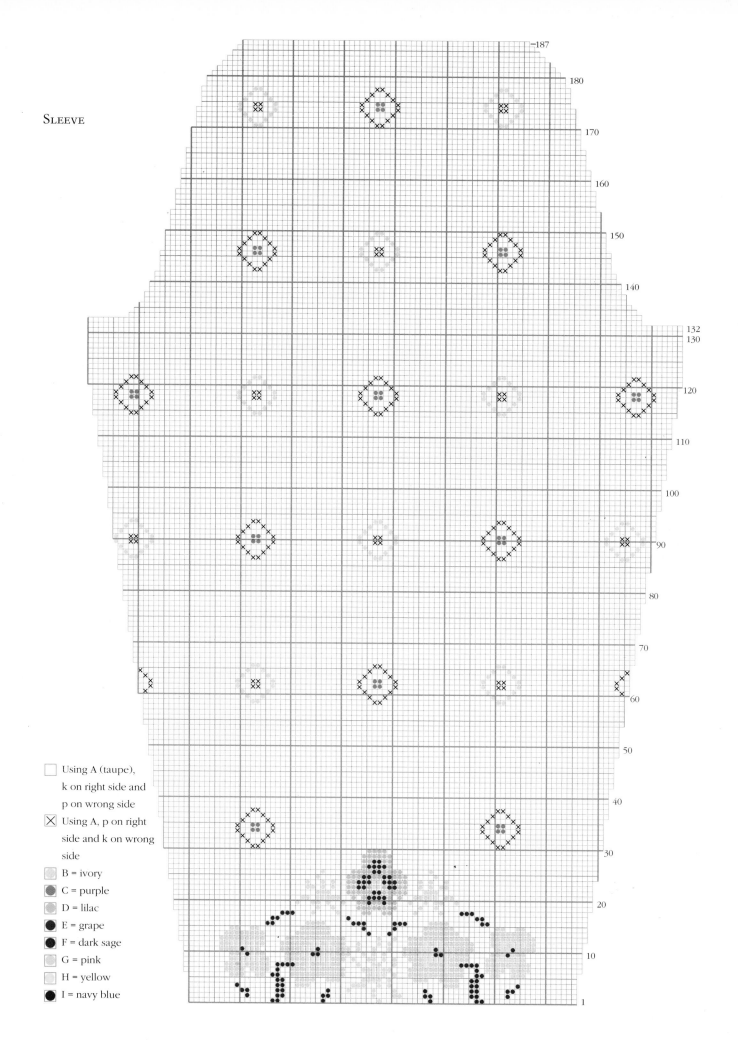

SLEEVE

Using A (taupe),
k on right side and
p on wrong side

☒ Using A, p on right
side and k on wrong
side

🔲 B = ivory

⬤ C = purple

⬤ D = lilac

⬤ E = grape

⬤ F = dark sage

🔲 G = pink

🔲 H = yellow

⬤ I = navy blue

18

BACK CHART C

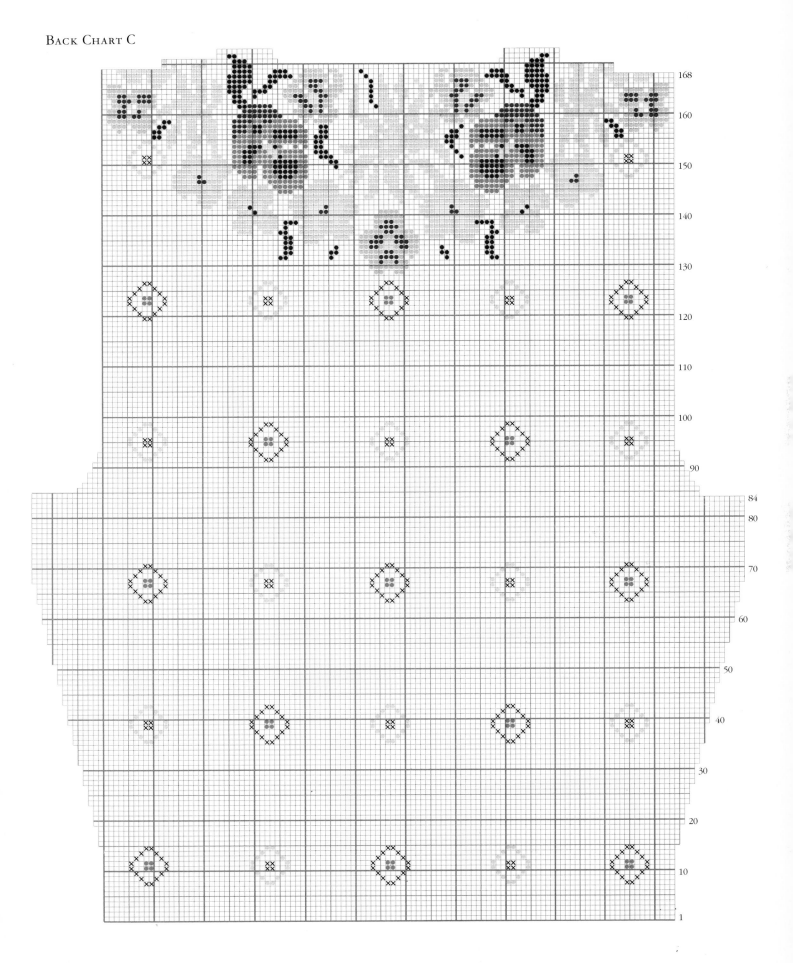

RIGHT FRONT
CHART E

LEFT FRONT
CHART D

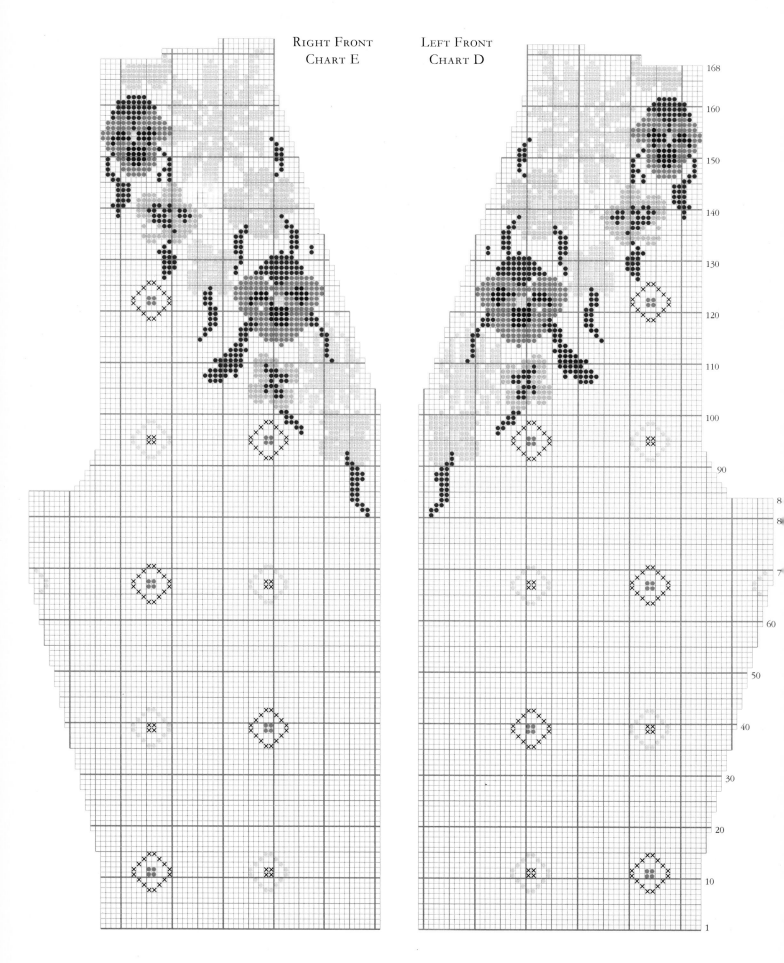

168
160
150
140
130
120
110
100
90
80
80
70
60
50
40
30
20
10
1

STRATFORD

HAVING KNITTED THIS SWEATER FOR MYSELF, I WEAR IT ALL

THE TIME IN SUMMER. THE SHAPE IS SO EASY TO WEAR AND THE

WONDERFULLY PRETTY SCULPTURED FAIR ISLE LOOKS

GOOD WITH ANYTHING.

MATERIALS
250g/8¾oz of a lightweight mercerised cotton in main colour A
50g/1¾oz each of contrast colours B, C, D, and E
Pair each of 2¼mm (US 1) and 3mm (US 3) knitting needles
1 spare 3mm (US 3) needle

MEASUREMENTS
Actual measurements
Bust 95cm/37½in
Length to shoulders 43cm/17in

TENSION/GAUGE
34 sts and 40 rows to 10cm/4in measured over patt worked on 3mm (US 3) needles

Please check your tension/gauge carefully and change needle size if necessary

NOTE
When working from chart use a 60cm/24in length of yarn for each isolated area of colour in B, C and D and twist yarns together at WS of work when changing colour to avoid making a hole.

BACK
Using smaller needles and A cast on 157 sts.
Rib row 1 (RS) K1, * p1, k1, rep from * to end.
Rib row 2 P1, * k1, p1, rep from * to end.
Rep these 2 ribbing rows for 4cm/1½in,
ending with a rib row 1.
Inc row Rib 27, * M1, rib 26, rep from * to end. 162 sts.
Change to larger needles. Beg with a k row, work 8 rows in st st.
Work in patt from chart as follows:
Row 9 (RS) Work last 9 sts of row 9, then work 24 st patt rep 6 times, then work first 9 sts of row 9.
Row 10 Work last 9 sts of row 10, then work 24 st patt rep 6 times, then work first 9 sts of row 10.
Cont in patt as set until back measures 16.5cm/6½in from cast-on edge, ending with a WS row.
Shape armholes
Keeping continuity of patt, cast/bind off 9 sts at beg of next 2 rows.
Cont straight until back measures 36cm/14¼in from cast-on edge, ending with a WS row.
*** Next row With larger needles patt 32 sts, then with smaller needles and A [k1, p1] 40 times, then with larger needles patt 32 sts.
Next row With larger needles patt 32 sts, then with smaller needles and A [p1, k1] 40 times, then with larger needles patt 32 sts.
Repeat these 2 rows 6 times more.
Shape neck
With larger needles patt 32 sts, then with smaller needles and A moss/seed st 11 sts, turn and leave rem sts on a spare needle.
** Cont straight on these sts until back

measures 43cm/17in from cast-on edge ending at armhole edge.

Shape shoulder

Keeping continuity of patt, cast/bind off 8 sts at beg of next and 3 foll alt rows.

Work 1 row.

Cast/bind off rem 11 sts. **

With right side facing, using smaller needles join A to rem sts and cast/bind off 58 sts, work in moss/seed st across next 10 sts, then using larger needles patt to end. 43 sts.

Complete to match first side from ** to **.

FRONT

Work as given for back until front measures 31cm/12¼in from beg ending with a WS row. Now work as given for back from ***

to end.

ARMBANDS

Join shoulder seams. With right side facing, using smaller needles and A pick up and k 189 sts evenly along row ends of armhole.

Patt row K1, * p1, k1, rep from * to end.

Rep this row for 5cm/2in.

Cast/bind off in patt.

FINISHING

Join first 10 rows of armbands to sts cast/bound off for armhole shaping. Join side and remainder of armband seams.

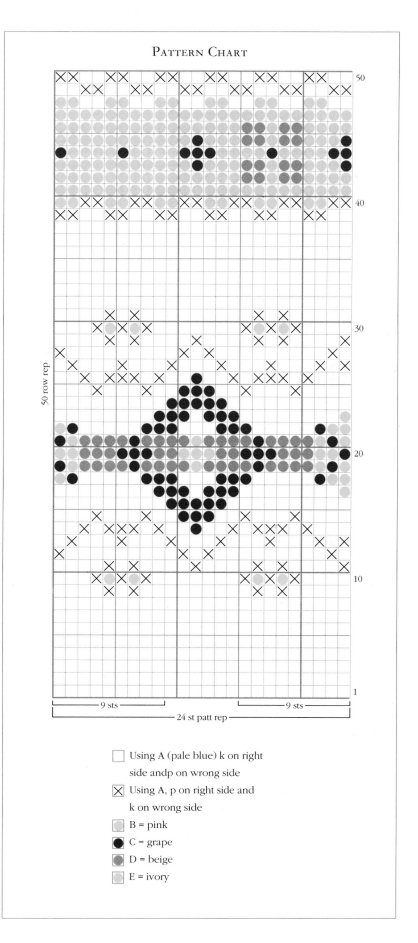

PATTERN CHART

50 row rep

9 sts   9 sts

24 st patt rep

☐ Using A (pale blue) k on right side and p on wrong side

☒ Using A, p on right side and k on wrong side

● B = pink

● C = grape

● D = beige

● E = ivory

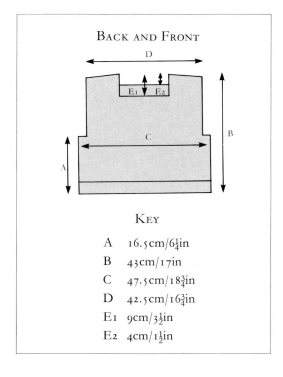

BACK AND FRONT

KEY

A   16.5cm/6¼in

B   43cm/17in

C   47.5cm/18¾in

D   42.5cm/16¾in

E1 9cm/3½in

E2 4cm/1½in

MONTICELLO

THE SHEEN OF SILK OR COTTON, COMBINED WITH THE ETHNIC

ROOTS OF THIS NAVAJO DESIGN, CREATES A SUPER SOPHISTICATED

SWEATER, GUARANTEED TO MAKE YOU FEEL A MILLION DOLLARS.

———————————◆———————————

MATERIALS
250g/8¾oz of a lightweight cotton in main colour A
100g/3½oz in contrast colour B
50g/1¾oz in each of contrast colours C, D, E, F and G
Pair each of 2¼mm (US 1) and 3¼mm (US 3) knitting needles
Set of 2¼mm (US 1) double pointed knitting needles

MEASUREMENTS
Actual measurements
Bust 90cm/35½in
Length to shoulders 53cm/20¾in
Sleeve seam 11.5cm/4½in

TENSION/GAUGE
32 sts and 38 rows to 10cm/4in measured over patt worked on 3¼mm (US 3) needles

Please check your tension/gauge carefully and change needle size if necessary

NOTE
When working from chart use separate small balls of yarn for each isolated area of colour and twist yarns together at WS of work when changing colour to avoid making a hole.

BACK
Using smaller needles and A cast on 103 sts.
Rib row 1 (RS) K1, * p1, k1, rep from *.

Rib row 2 P1, * k1, p1, rep from * to end.
Rep these 2 rows for 1.5cm/½in ending with rib row 1.
Inc row Rib 1, * M1, rib 2, M1, rib 3, rep from * to last 2 sts, M1, rib 2. 144 sts.
Change to larger needles. Beg with a k row and working in st st, work 7 rows B and 6 rows A.
Work in st st in patt from chart as foll:
Row 14 (WS) Work last 8 sts of row 14, then work 32 st patt rep 4 times, then work first 8 sts of row 14.
Row 15 Work last 8 sts of row 15, then work 32 st patt rep 4 times, then work first 8 sts of row 15.
Cont in patt as set until back measures 21.5cm/8½in from cast-on edge, ending with a WS row.
Make a note on chart of the next patt row to be worked.
Cont in patt until back measures 31.5cm/12½in from cast-on edge ending with a WS row.
Shape armholes
Keep continuity of patt, cast/bind off 8 sts at beg of next 2 rows.
Dec 1 st at each end of the next and every foll alt row until 116 sts rem.
Cont straight until back measures 43cm/17in from cast-on edge, ending with a WS row.
Shape neck
Next row Patt 34 sts, turn and leave rem sts on a spare needle.

** Dec 1 st at neck edge on next and every foll alt row until 20 sts rem.

Cont straight until back measures 53cm/20¾in from cast-on edge ending at armhole edge.

Shape shoulder

Cast/bind off 10 sts at beg of next row.

Work 1 row.

Cast/bind off rem 10 sts. **

With right side facing slip next 48 sts of rem sts on to a spare needle, join on yarn, patt to end.

Complete to match first side from ** to **.

FRONT

Work as given for back until front measures 40.5cm/16in from beg ending with a WS row.

Shape neck

Next row Patt 38 sts, turn and leave rem sts on a spare needle.

*** Dec 1 st at neck edge on next and every foll alt row until 20 sts rem.

Cont straight until front measures the same as back to shoulder ending at armhole edge.

Shape shoulder

Cast/bind off 10 sts at beg of next row.

Work 1 row.

Cast/bind off rem 10 sts. ***

With right side facing slip next 40 sts of rem sts on to a spare needle, join on yarn, patt to end.

Complete to match first side from *** to ***.

SLEEVES

Using smaller needles and A cast on 87 sts. Work 1.5cm/½in rib as given for back, ending with a RS row.

Inc row Rib 3, M1, rib 2, rep from * to last 4 sts, M1, rib 4. 128 sts.

Change to larger needles and work from chart as follows.

Starting with the row noted when working the back work the 32 sts of patt rep 4 times.

Cont in patt until sleeve measures 11.5cm/4½in from cast-on edge ending with same patt row as back before armhole shaping.

Shape top

Cast/bind off 8 sts at beg of next 2 rows.

Dec 1 st at each end of the next and every foll alt row until 48 sts rem.

Cast/bind off tightly.

NECKBAND

Join shoulder seams.

Using 3 of the double pointed needles and A, starting at left shoulder, pick up and k 48 sts evenly down left side of front neck, k across 40 sts from front neck holder, pick up and k 48 sts up right side of front neck, pick up and k 38 sts down right side of back neck, k across 48 sts from back neck holder, pick up and k 38 sts up left side of back neck. 260 sts.

Work in rounds of k1, p1 rib for 1.5cm/½in. Cast/bind off in rib.

FINISHING

Set in sleeves. Join side and sleeve seams.

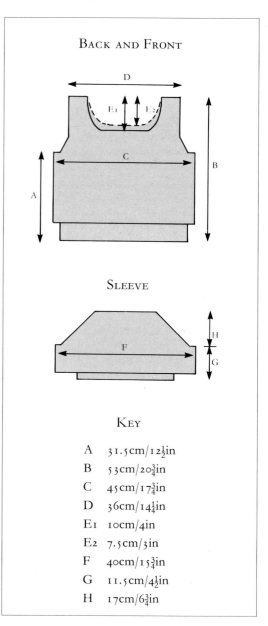

BACK AND FRONT

SLEEVE

KEY

A 31.5cm/12½in
B 53cm/20¾in
C 45cm/17¾in
D 36cm/14¼in
E1 10cm/4in
E2 7.5cm/3in
F 40cm/15¾in
G 11.5cm/4½in
H 17cm/6¾in

PATTERN CHART

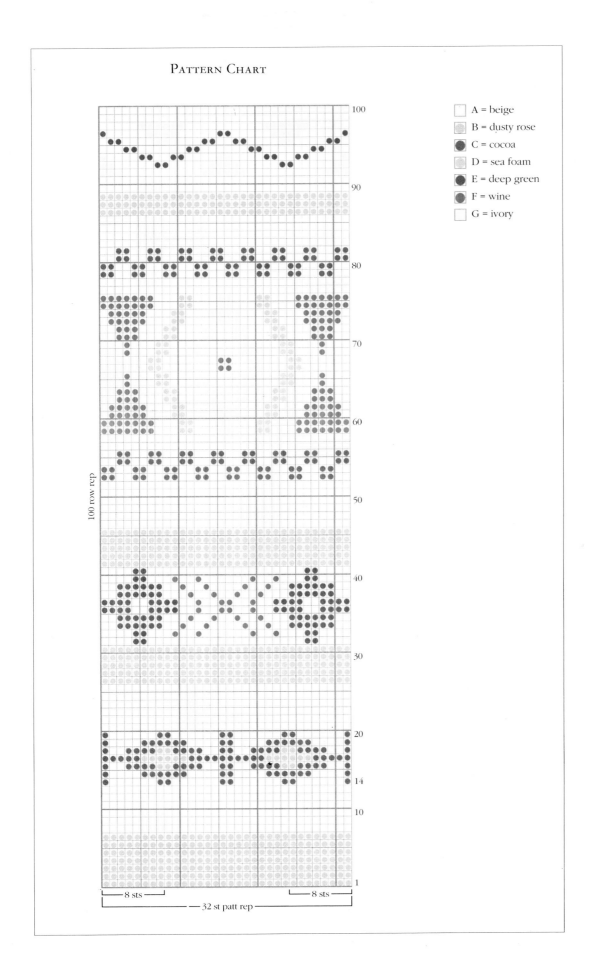

A = beige
B = dusty rose
C = cocoa
D = sea foam
E = deep green
F = wine
G = ivory

100 row rep

8 sts   8 sts
32 st patt rep

C H A N T I L L Y

I LOVE THE JUXTAPOSITION OF ARAN PATTERNS WITH

LIGHTWEIGHT, SUMMER SHAPES. IT IS A WELCOME CHALLENGE TO

USE THE OLD, WELL-TRIED PATTERNS IN STUNNING NEW WAYS.

MATERIALS
100g/3½oz of a lightweight soft cotton
Pair each of 2¾mm (US 2) and 3¼mm (US 3) knitting needles
Cable needle
2.50mm (US C) crochet hook

MEASUREMENTS
Actual measurements
Bust 72cm/28¼in
Length to underarm 30.5cm/12in

TENSION/GAUGE
26 sts and 34 rows to 10cm/4in measured over patt worked on 3¼mm (US 3) needles

Please check your tension/gauge carefully and change needle size if necessary

Pattern No 1 (worked over 14 sts)
Row 1 P1, k12, p1.
Row 2 K1, p12, k1.
Rows 3 and 4 As rows 1 and 2.
Row 5 P1, C6B (see page 159), C6F, p1.
Row 6 K1, p12, k1.
These 6 rows form the patt and are repeated throughout.

Pattern No 2 (worked over 11 sts)
Row 1 (RS) P2, [k1 tbl, p1] 4 times, p1.
Row 2 K2, [p1, k1] 4 times, k1.
Rows 3 to 6 Rep rows 1 and 2 twice more.
Row 7 P2, slip next 4 sts on to cable needle and leave at front of work, [k1 tbl, p1] twice, [k1 tbl, p1] twice from cable needle, p1.
Row 8 As row 2.
Rows 9 and 10 As rows 1 and 2.
These 10 rows form the patt and are repeated throughout.

Pattern No 3 (worked over 35 sts)
Row 1 K5, k1 tbl, p1, [k1 tbl] 3 times, p1, k1 tbl, k11, k1 tbl, p1, [k1 tbl] 3 times, p1, k1 tbl, k5.
Row 2 P5, p1 tbl, k1, [p1 tbl] 3 times, k1, p1 tbl, p11, p1 tbl, k1, [p1 tbl] 3 times, k1, p1 tbl, p5.
Row 3 K4, [Cr2Rp] twice, k1 tbl, [Cr2Lp] twice, k9, [Cr2Rp] twice, k1 tbl, [Cr2Lp] twice, k4.
Row 4 P4, [p1 tbl, k1] 4 times, p1 tbl, p9, [p1 tbl, k1] 4 times, p1 tbl, p4.
Row 5 K3, [Cr2Rp] twice, [k1 tbl] 3 times, [Cr2Lp] twice, k7, [Cr2Rp] twice, [k1 tbl] 3 times, [Cr2Lp] twice, k3.
Row 6 P3, [p1 tbl, k1] twice, [p1 tbl] 3 times, [k1, p1 tbl] twice, p7, [p1 tbl, k1] twice, [p1 tbl] 3 times, [k1, p1 tbl] twice, p3.
Row 7 K2, [Cr2Rp] 3 times, k1 tbl, [Cr2Lp] 3 times, k5, [Cr2Rp] 3 times, k1 tbl, [Cr2Lp] 3 times, k2.
Row 8 P2, [p1 tbl, k1] 6 times, p1 tbl, p5, [p1 tbl, k1] 6 times, p1 tbl, p2.
Row 9 K1, [Cr2Rp] 3 times, [k1 tbl] 3 times, [Cr2Lp] 3 times, k3, [Cr2Lp] 3 times, [k1 tbl] 3 times, [Cr2Rp] 3 times, k1.

Row 10 P1, [p1 tbl, k1] 3 times, [p1 tbl] 3 times, [k1, p1 tbl] 3 times, p3, [p1 tbl, k1] 3 times, [p1 tbl] 3 times, [k1, p1 tbl] 3 times, p1.

Row 11 [Cr2Rp] 4 times, k1 tbl, [Cr2Lp] 4 times, k1 tbl, [Cr2Rp] 4 times, k1 tbl, [Cr2Lp] 4 times.

Row 12 [P1 tbl, k1] 8 times, [p1 tbl] 3 times, [k1, p1 tbl] 8 times.

Row 13 Cr2L, [Cr2Lp] 3 times, k1 tbl, [Cr2R] 4 times, k1 tbl, [Cr2Lp] 4 times, k1 tbl, [Cr2Rp] 3 times, Cr2R.

Row 14 P1, [p1 tbl, k1] 3 times, [p1 tbl] 3 times, [k1, p1 tbl] 8 times, [p1 tbl] twice, [k1, p1 tbl] 3 times, p1.

Row 15 K1, Cr2L, [Cr2Lp] twice, p1, k1 tbl, p1, [Cr2Rp] 3 times, [k1 tbl] 3 times, [Cr2Lp] 3 times, p1, k1 tbl, p1, [Cr2Rp] twice, Cr2R, k1.

Row 16 P2, [p1 tbl, k1] 7 times, [p1 tbl] 3 times, [k1, p1 tbl] 7 times, p2.

Row 17 K2, Cr2L, [Cr2Lp] twice, k1 tbl, [Cr2Rp] 4 times, k1 tbl, [Cr2Lp] 4 times, k1 tbl, [Cr2Rp] twice, Cr2R, k2.

Row 18 P3, [p1 tbl, k1] twice, [p1 tbl] 3 times, [k1, p1 tbl] 8 times, [p1 tbl] twice, [k1, p1 tbl] twice, p3.

Row 19 K3, Cr2L, Cr2Lp, p1, k1 tbl, p1, [Cr2Rp] 3 times, [k1 tbl] 3 times, [Cr2Lp] 3 times, p1, k1 tbl, p1, Cr2Rp, Cr2R, k3.

Row 20 P4, [p1 tbl, k1] 6 times, [p1 tbl] 3 times, [k1, p1 tbl] 6 times, p4.

Row 21 K4, Cr2L, Cr2Lp, k1 tbl, [Cr2Rp] 4 times, k1 tbl, [Cr2Lp] 4 times, k1 tbl, Cr2Rp, Cr2R, k4.

Row 22 P5, p1 tbl, k1, [p1 tbl] 3 times, [k1, p1 tbl] 7 times, k1 [p1 tbl] 3 times, k1, p1 tbl, p5.

Row 23 K5, Cr2L, p1, k1 tbl, p1, [Cr2Rp] 3 times, [k1 tbl] 3 times, [Cr2Lp] 3 times, p1, k1 tbl, p1, Cr2R, k5.

Row 24 P6, [p1 tbl, k1] 5 times, [p1 tbl] 3 times, [k1, p1 tbl] 5 times, p6.

Row 25 K6, Cr2L, k1 tbl, [Cr2Rp] 4 times, k1 tbl, [Cr2Lp] 4 times, k1 tbl, Cr2R, k6.

Row 26 P7, [p1 tbl] 3 times, [k1, p1 tbl] 7 times, k1, [p1 tbl] 3 times, p7.

Row 27 K6, Cr2Rp, k1 tbl, Cr2Lp, p1, [Cr2Rp] twice, [k1 tbl] 3 times, [Cr2Lp] twice, p1, Cr2Rp, k1 tbl, Cr2Lp, k6.

Row 28 As row 24.

Row 29 K5, Cr2Rp, [k1 tbl] 3 times, Cr2L,

p1, [Cr2Rp] twice, k1 tbl, [Cr2Lp] twice, p1, Cr2Rp, [k1 tbl] 3 times, Cr2Lp, ending with k5.

Row 30 As row 22.

Row 31 K4, [Cr2Rp] twice, k1 tbl, [Cr2Lp] twice, p1, Cr2Rp, [k1 tbl] 3 times, Cr2Lp, p1, [Cr2Rp] twice, k1 tbl, [Cr2Lp] twice, k4.

Row 32 As row 20.

Row 33 K3, [Cr2Rp] twice, [k1 tbl] 3 times, [Cr2Lp] twice, p1, Cr2Rp, k1 tbl, Cr2Lp, slip next st on to cable needle and hold at front of work, p1, place st on cable needle at back of work, k1 tbl, p st from cable needle, Cr2Rp, [k1 tbl] 3 times, [Cr2Lp] twice, k3.

Row 34 As row 18.

Row 35 K2, [Cr2Rp] 3 times, k1 tbl, [Cr2Lp] 3 times, p2, k1 tbl, p2, [Cr2Rp] 3 times, k1 tbl, [Cr2Lp] 3 times, k2.

Row 36 P2, [p1 tbl, k1] 6 times, [p1 tbl, k2] twice, [p1 tbl, k1] 6 times, p1 tbl, p2.

Row 37 K1, [Cr2Rp] 3 times, [k1 tbl] 3 times, [Cr2Lp] 3 times, p1, k1 tbl, p1, [Cr2Rp] 3 times, [k1 tbl] 3 times, [Cr2Lp] 3 times, k1.

Row 38 P1, [p1 tbl, k1] 3 times, [p1 tbl] 3 times, [k1, p1 tbl] 3 times, k1, p1 tbl, k1, [p1 tbl, k1] 3 times, [p1 tbl] 3 times, [k1, p1 tbl] 3 times, p1.

Rows 11 to 38 form the patt and are repeated throughout.

BACK
Using smaller needles cast on 84 sts.

Rib row 1 (RS) [K1, p1] 3 times, * p3, [k1 tbl] 3 times, p3 *, rep from * to * 7 times more, [p1, k1] 3 times.

Rib row 2 [P1, k1] 3 times, * k3, [p1 tbl] 3

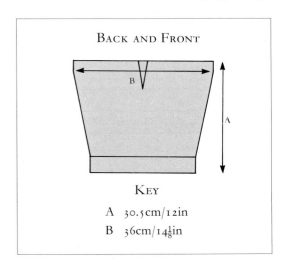

BACK AND FRONT

KEY

A   30.5cm/12in

B   36cm/14⅛in

times, k3 *, rep from * to * 7 times more, [k1, p1] 3 times.

Rib row 3 (RS) [K1, p1] 3 times, * p2, Cr2Rp, k1 tbl, Cr2Lp, p2 *, rep from * to * 7 times more, [p1, k1] 3 times.

Rib row 4 [P1, k1] 3 times, * k2, [p1 tbl, k1] twice, p1 tbl, k2 *, rep from * to * 7 times more, [k1, p1] 3 times.

Rib row 5 (RS) [K1, p1] 3 times. * p1, Cr2Rp, p1, k1 tbl, p1, Cr2Lp, p1 *, rep from * to * 7 times more, [p1, k1] 3 times.

Rib row 6 [P1, k1] 3 times, * k1, [p1 tbl, k2] twice, p1 tbl, k1 *, rep from * to * 7 times more, [k1, p1] 3 times.

Rib row 7 (RS) [K1, p1] 3 times, * Cr2Rp, p1, [k1 tbl] 3 times, p1, Cr2Lp *, rep from * to * 7 times more, [p1, k1] 3 times.

Rib row 8 [P1, k1] 3 times, * p1 tbl, k2, [p1 tbl] 3 times, k2, p1 tbl *, rep from * to * 7 times more, [k1, p1] 3 times.

Rep these 8 rows for 4cm/1½in ending with a RS row.

Inc row Patt 7, * M1, patt 7, rep from * to end. 95 sts.

Change to larger needles.

Work in patt as follows:

Row 1 For moss/seed st p1, k1, then p1, k1, p1, work row 1 of pattern No 1 over next 14 sts, work row 1 of pattern No 2 over next 11 sts, work row 1 of pattern No 3 over next 35 sts, work row 1 of pattern No 2 over next 11 sts, work row 1 of pattern No 1 over next 14 sts, p1, k1, p1, for moss/seed st k1, p1.

Row 2 For moss/seed st p1, k1, then k1, p1, k1, work row 2 of pattern No 1 over next 14 sts, work row 2 of pattern No 2 over next 11 sts, work row 2 of pattern No 3 over next 35 sts, work row 2 of pattern No 2 over next 11 sts, work row 2 of pattern No 1 over next 14 sts, k1, p1, k1, for moss/seed st k1, p1.

These 2 rows set the patt.

Cont in patt inc and work into moss/seed st at sides 1 st at each end of the 5th and every foll 7th row until there are 119 sts.

Work straight until work measures 29cm/11½in from cast-on edge ending with a WS row.

Increasing 1 st at each end and 1 st in the centre, k 1 row. 122 sts. P 1 row.

Next row K1, yo, * k5, turn, lift 2nd, 3rd, 4th and 5th sts over first st and off the needle, turn, yo, rep from * to last st, k1.

Next row P1, * [p1, yo, k1 tbl] all into next st, p1, rep from * to end.

Next row K2, * k1 tbl, k3, rep from * to last 3 sts, k1 tbl, k2.

Cast/bind off.

FRONT

Work as given for back until work measures 25cm/9¾in from beg ending with a RS row.

Front opening

Next row Patt 59 sts, cast/bind off next st, patt to end.

Next row Patt 59 sts, turn and leave rem sts on a spare needle.

Cont straight until front measures 29cm/11½in from cast-on edge ending with the same patt row as back.

Increasing 1 st at each end and 1 st in the centre, k 1 row. 62 sts. P 1 row.

Next row K1, yo, * k5, turn, lift 2nd, 3rd, 4th and 5th sts over first st and off the needle, turn, yo, rep from * to last st, k1.

Next row P1, * [p1, yo, k1 tbl] all into next st, p1, rep from * to end.

Next row K2, * k1 tbl, k3, rep from * to last 3 sts, k1 tbl, k2.

Cast/bind off.

With right side facing return to sts on spare needle, join on yarn and patt to end.

Complete to match first side.

TOP EDGING

Join side seams.

Join yarn to top of left side seam, with crochet hook work 1 slip st in same place as join, * miss next 2 sts, 5 tr/dc (see page 159) in next st, miss next 2 sts, 1 slip st in next st, rep from * to corner, work in dc/sc around opening to next corner, rep from * to left side seam. Fasten off.

STRAPS (make 2)

Make a ch 38cm/15in long, work 1 dc/sc into each ch. Fasten off. Sew straps inside shell border to fit.

CORD

Make a ch 130cm/51in long, work 1 dc/sc into each ch. Fasten off.

Thread cord through holes to tie at centre front.

EVESHAM

THIS IS ANOTHER SWEATER FROM MY ART DECO COLLECTION.

THE TRELLIS IS A THEME I LOVE TO WORK WITH AND PROVIDES A

WONDERFUL BACKDROP FOR THE STYLISED DECO FLOWERS.

MATERIALS
300g/10½oz of a 4 ply (US sport weight) botany wool in main colour A
50g/1¾oz each of contrast colours B, C, D, E and F
Pair each of 2¼mm (US 1) and 3¼mm (US 3) knitting needles
1 spare 3¼mm (US 3) needle

MEASUREMENTS
Actual measurements
Bust 90cm/35½in
Length to shoulders 53cm/21in
Sleeve seam 41cm/16¼in

TENSION/GAUGE
30 sts and 42 rows to 10cm/4in measured over patt worked on 3¼mm (US 3) needles

Please check your tension/gauge carefully and change needle size if necessary

NOTE
When working from charts use separate small balls of yarn for each isolated area of colour and twist yarns together at WS of work when changing colour to avoid making a hole.

BACK
Using smaller needles and A cast on 122 sts.
Rib row 1 (RS) K2, * p2, k2, rep from * to end.
Rib row 2 P2, * k2, p2, rep from * to end.

Rep these 2 rows for 13cm/5in ending with rib row 1.
Inc row Rib 9, * M1, rib 8, rep from * to last 9 sts, M1, rib 9. 136 sts.
Change to larger needles.
Work in patt from chart until row 74 has been worked.
Shape armholes
Cast/bind off 4 sts at beg of next 2 rows.
Dec 1 st at each end of the next 4 rows and the 3 foll alt rows. 114 sts.
Cont straight from chart until row 144 has been worked.
** Next row With larger needles patt 24 sts from chart, then with smaller needles [k1, p1] 33 times, then with larger needles patt 24 sts from chart.
Next row With larger needles patt 24 sts from chart, then with smaller needles [p1, k1] 33 times, then with larger needles patt 24 sts from chart.
Repeat these 2 rows 5 times more.
Shape neck
With larger needles patt 24 sts, then with smaller needles moss/seed st 11 sts, turn and leave rem sts on a spare needle.
Cont straight on these sts until row 168 has been worked.
Shape shoulder
Keeping continuity of patt, cast/bind off 11 sts at beg of next row and 10 sts on the foll alt row.
Work 1 row.

Cast/bind off rem 14 sts.
With right side facing, using smaller needles join yarn to rem sts, cast/bind off 44 sts, work in moss/seed st across next 10 sts, then using larger needles patt to end. 35 sts.
Cont straight on these sts until row 169 has been worked.

Shape shoulder
Keeping continuity of patt, cast/bind off 11 sts at beg of next row and 10 sts on the foll alt row.
Cast/bind off rem 14 sts.

FRONT
Work as given for back until row 128 has been worked.
Now work as given for back from ** to end.

SLEEVES
Using smaller needles and A cast on 54 sts. Work 9cm/3½in rib as given for back, ending with a RS row.
In row Rib 6, * M1, rib 4, rep from * to end. 66 sts.
Change to larger needles and work from chart, shaping sides of sleeves as shown.

FINISHING
Join shoulder seams. Set in sleeves. Join side and sleeve seams.

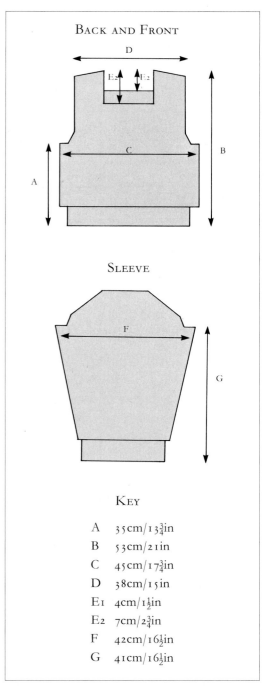

BACK AND FRONT

SLEEVE

KEY

A   35cm/13¾in
B   53cm/21in
C   45cm/17¾in
D   38cm/15in
E1   4cm/1½in
E2   7cm/2¾in
F   42cm/16½in
G   41cm/16½in

SLEEVE

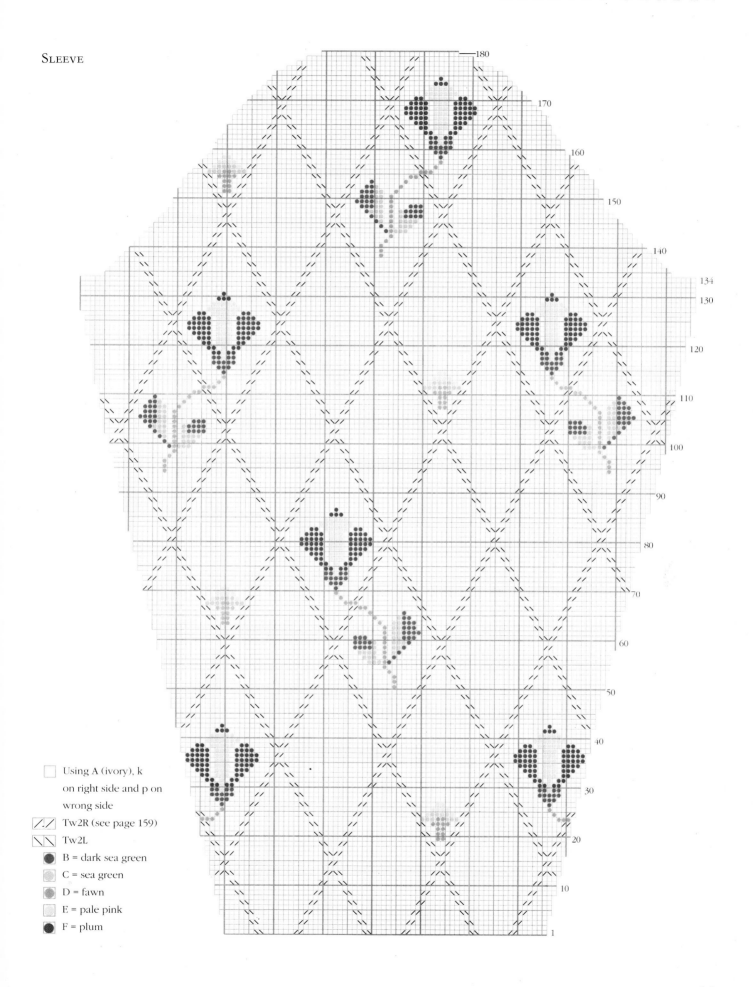

Using A (ivory), k
on right side and p on
wrong side

Tw2R (see page 159)

Tw2L

B = dark sea green

C = sea green

D = fawn

E = pale pink

F = plum

Country Garden

Back and Front

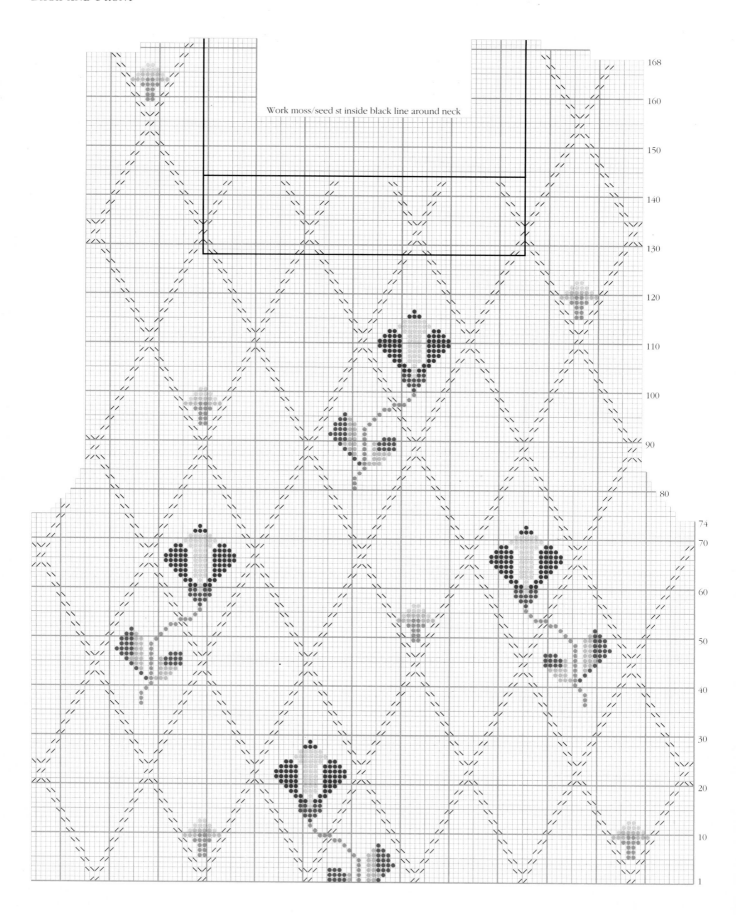

Work moss/seed st inside black line around neck

CHARLESTON

WITH THIS SWEATER I WANTED TO EXPRESS THE BOLD,

FREE USE OF COLOUR SEEN IN THE ART DECO MOVEMENT, AND

IN PARTICULAR IN THE POTTERY OF CLARICE CLIFF.

◆

MATERIALS
750g/26½oz of a double knitting (US worsted weight) wool in main colour A
50g/1¾oz each of contrast colours B, C, D, E, F, G and H
Pair each of 3mm (US 2) and 4mm (US 6) knitting needles
8 buttons

MEASUREMENTS
Actual measurements
Bust 105cm/41½in
Length to shoulders 69.5cm/27¼in
Sleeve length (adjustable) 53cm/21in

TENSION/GAUGE
24 sts and 30 rows to 10cm/4in measured over st st worked on 4mm (US 6) needles

Please check your tension/gauge carefully and change needle size if necessary

NOTE
When working from charts use separate small balls of yarn for each isolated area of colour and twist yarns together at WS of work when changing colour to avoid making a hole.

BACK
Using smaller needles and A cast on 121 sts.
Rib row 1 (RS) K1, * p1, k1, rep from * to end.
Rib row 2 P1, * k1, p1, rep from * to end.

Rep these 2 rows for 2.5cm/1in ending with rib row 1.
Inc row Rib 21, * M1, rib 20, rep from * to end. 126 sts.
Change to larger needles.
Work in patt from chart for back for 126 rows.
Shape armholes
Cast/bind off 3 sts at beg of next 2 rows.
Cont in patt from chart until row 201 has been worked.
Shape shoulders
Cast/bind off 42 sts, work in patt until there are 36 sts on the needle, cast/bind off rem 42 sts. Leave 36 sts on spare needle for back neck.

POCKET LININGS (make 2)
Using larger needles and A cast on 30 sts.
Work 13cm/5in in st st ending with a k row.
Leave these sts on a holder

LEFT FRONT
Using smaller needles and A cast on 71 sts.
Rib row 1 (RS) * P1, k1, rep from * to last 3 sts, p1, k2.
Rib row 2 K1, * p1, k1, rep from * to end.
Rep these 2 rows for 2.5 cm/1in ending with rib row 1.
Inc row Rib across first 14 sts, then slip these sts on to a safety pin, then rib 15, * M1, rib 14, rep from * to end. 60 sts.
Change to larger needles.

Work in patt from chart for left front for 37 rows.

Place pocket

Row 38 P15 sts, slip next 30 sts on to a holder, p across 30 sts of one pocket lining, one then p to end.

Cont in patt from chart until row 126 has been worked.

Shape armhole

Cast/bind off 3 sts at beg of next row.

Cont in patt from chart until row 179 has been worked.

Shape neck

Cast/bind off 5 sts at beg of next row.

Dec 2 sts at neck edge on next 2 rows then 1 st on foll 3 rows. Dec 1 st at neck edge on 3 foll alt rows. 42 sts.

Cont working from chart until row 202 has been worked. Cast/bind off.

RIGHT FRONT

Using smaller needles and A cast on 71 sts.

Rib row 1 (RS) K2, * P1, k1, rep from * to last st, p1.

Rib row 2 K1, * p1, k1, rep from * to end.

Rep these 2 rows once more.

Buttohnhole row 1 Rib 5, cast/bind off 4 sts, rib to end.

Buttonhole row 2 Rib to end, casting on 4 sts over those cast/bound off in previous row.

Cont in rib until ribbing measures 2.5 cm/1 in ending with rib row 1.

Inc row Rib 15, * M1, rib 14, rep from * twice more, slip rem 14 sts on to a safety pin. 60 sts.

Change to larger needles.

Complete in patt foll chart for right front for shaping.

SLEEVES

Using smaller needles and A cast on 51 sts. Work 2.5 cm/1 in rib as given for back, ending with a RS row.

Inc row Rib 1, * M1, rib 3, rep from * to last 2 sts, M1, rib 2. 68 sts.

Change to larger needles

Work in patt from chart for sleeves, increasing 1 st at each end of rows as shown.

When row 152 has been worked, cast/bind off.

BUTTON BAND

With right side facing, slip sts from safety pin on to a smaller needle, join on A and cont in rib until band is long enough, when slightly stretched, to fit up left front to neck shaping, ending with a WS row. Break off yarn and slip these sts on to a safety pin. Sew band in place. Sew on buttons, the first level with buttonhole already worked, the 7th 5.5 cm/2¼ in below neckline, and 5 more spaced evenly between these two.

BUTTONHOLE BAND

With wrong side facing, slip sts from safety pin on to a smaller needle, join on A and cont

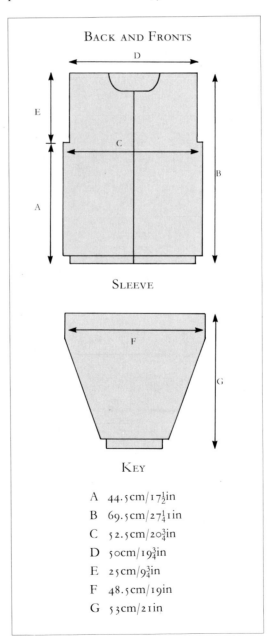

BACK AND FRONTS

SLEEVE

KEY

A 44.5 cm/17½ in
B 69.5 cm/27¼1 in
C 52.5 cm/20¾ in
D 50 cm/19¾ in
E 25 cm/9¾ in
F 48.5 cm/19 in
G 53 cm/21 in

in rib as for button band making button-holes to correspond with buttons as follows:
Buttonhole row 1 (RS) Rib 5, cast/bind off 4 sts, rib to end.
Buttonhole row 2 Rib to end, casting on 4 sts over those cast/bound off in previous row.
Do not break off yarn at end.

NECKBAND
Join shoulder seams.
With right side facing using smaller needles and A, rib across 14 sts of buttonhole band, pick up and k 30 sts up right side of front neck, k across 36 sts from holder at back neck, pick up and k 29 sts down left side of front neck, rib across 14 sts of buttonhole band. 123 sts.
Work 3 rows rib as set.

Buttonhole row 1 (RS) Rib 5, cast/bind off 4 sts, rib to end.
Buttonhole row 2 Rib to end, casting on 4 sts over those cast/bound off in previous row.
Work 4 more rows in rib.
Cast/bind off in rib.

POCKET TOPS
With right side facing using smaller needles and A, increasing 1 st at centre k across sts from holder. 31 sts.
Work 5 rows rib as given for back.
Cast/bind off in rib.

FINISHING
Set in sleeves. Join side and sleeve seams.
Sew pockets and row ends of pocket ribs in place. Sew on rem button.

SLEEVE

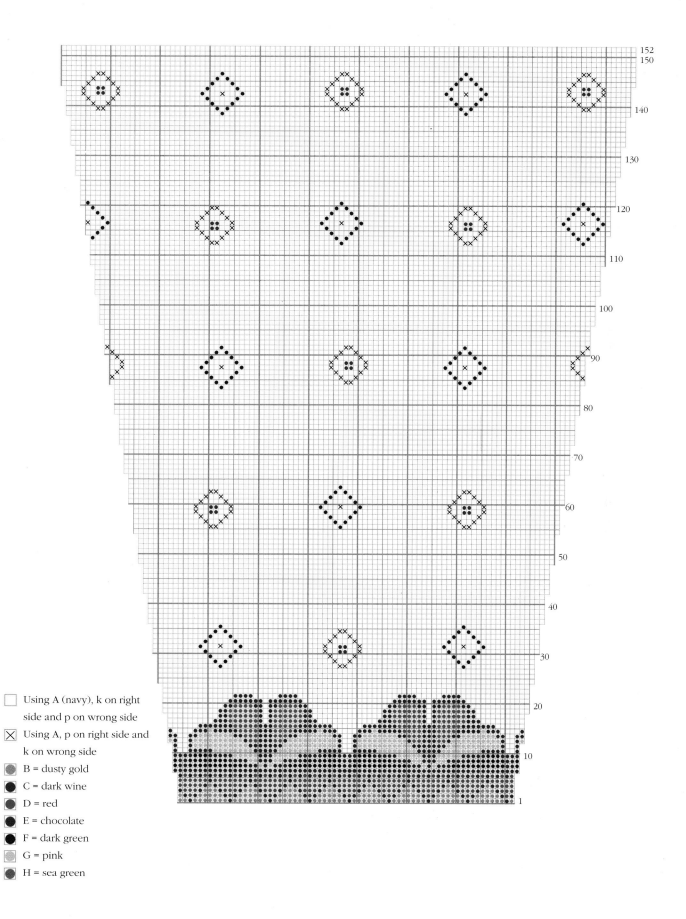

152
150
140
130
120
110
100
90
80
70
60
50
40
30
20
10
1

☐ Using A (navy), k on right
side and p on wrong side

☒ Using A, p on right side and
k on wrong side

◉ B = dusty gold

● C = dark wine

● D = red

● E = chocolate

● F = dark green

◉ G = pink

◉ H = sea green

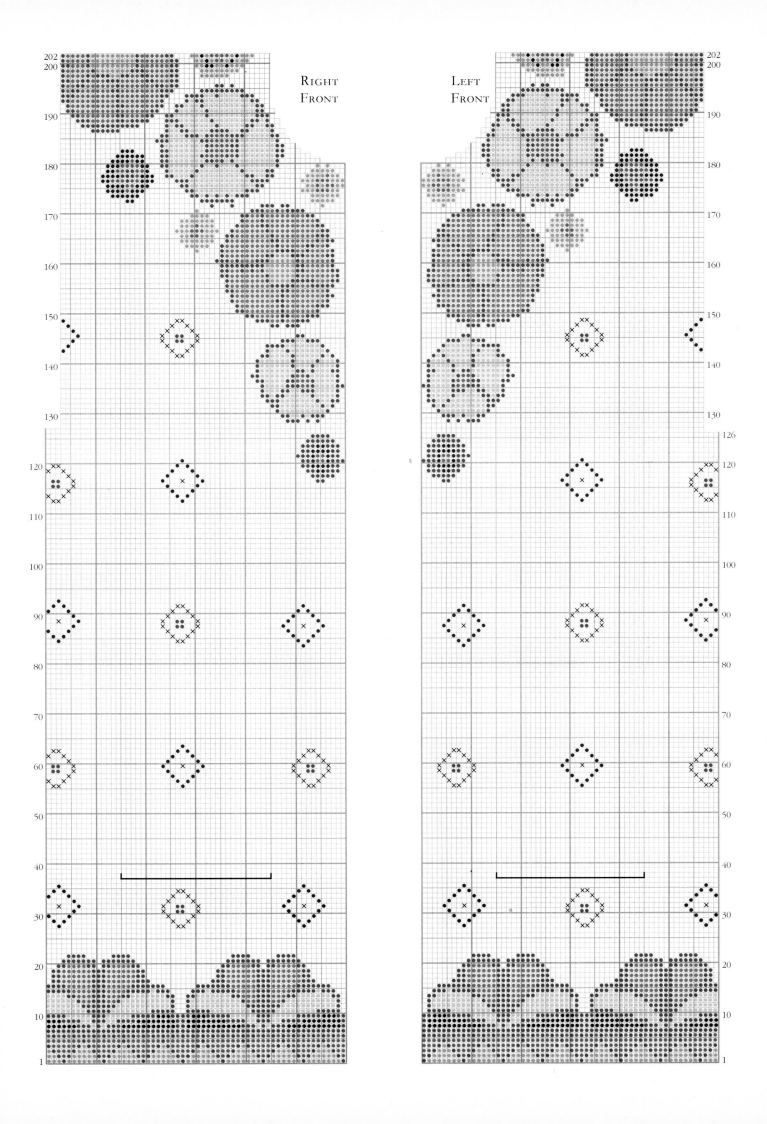

RIGHT
FRONT

LEFT
FRONT

ROSEDALE

A WONDERFUL SWEATER FOR AFTERNOON TEA IN THE GARDEN,

THIS IS INSPIRED BY THE PALM COURT TEA DANCES OF THE

TWENTIES AND THIRTIES.

---◆---

MATERIALS
350g/12½oz of a lightweight soft cotton
Pair each of 2¼mm (US 1) and 3¼mm (US 3)
knitting needles
Cable needle
5 buttons

MEASUREMENTS
Actual measurements
Bust 101cm/39½in
Length to shoulders 48cm/19in
Sleeve seam 13cm/5in

TENSION/GAUGE
32 sts and 36 rows to 10cm/4in measured
over patt worked on 3¼mm (US 3) needles

***Please check your tension/gauge carefully
and change needle size if necessary***

BACK
Using smaller needles cast on 87 sts.
Patt row (RS) K1, * p1, k1, rep from *.
Rep this row for 2cm/¾in, ending with a RS
row.
Inc row Patt 2, * M1, patt 1, M1, patt 2, rep
from * to last st, M1, patt 1. 144 sts.
Change to larger needles and patt.
Row 1 K1, * p2, k6, p2, k1, rep from * to
end.
Row 2 P1, * k2, p6, k2, p1, rep from * to end.
Rows 3 and 4 As rows 1 and 2.
Row 5 K1, * p2, C6F (see page 159), p2, k1,

p2, k6, p2, k1, rep from * to last 11 sts, p2,
C6F, p2, k1.
Row 6 As row 2.
Row 7 As row 1.
Row 8 As row 2.
Row 9 to 16 Rep rows 5 to 8 twice more.
Row 17 K1, * p2, k6, p2, k1, p2, C6F, p2, k1,
rep from * to last 11 sts, p2, k6, p2, k1.
Row 18 As row 2.
Row 19 As row 1.
Row 20 As row 2.
Rows 21 to 28 Rep rows 17 to 20 twice
more.
Rows 5 to 28 form the patt and are repeated
throughout.
Inc and work into patt 1 st at each end of the
next and every foll 6th row until there are
162 sts.
Work straight until back measures 28cm/
11in from cast-on edge, ending with a WS
row.
Shape armholes
Cast/bind off 8 sts at beg of next 2 rows.
Dec 1 st at each end of every row until 124 sts
rem.
Cont straight in patt until back measures
43cm/17in from cast-on edge, ending with a
WS row.
Dec row K5, * k2 tog, k2, rep from * to last
7 sts, k2 tog, k5. 95 sts.
Cont in moss/seed st until back measures
48cm/19in from cast-on edge, ending with a
WS row.

Shape shoulders

Cast/bind off 9 sts at beg of next 6 rows and 8 sts at beg of foll 2 rows.
Cast/bind off rem 25 sts.

LEFT FRONT

Using smaller needles cast on 41 sts.
Patt row (RS) K1, * p1, k1, rep from * to end.
Rep this row for 2cm/¾in, ending with a RS row.
Inc row Patt 3, * M1, patt 1, M1, patt 2, rep from * to last 2 sts, M1, patt 2. 66 sts.
Change to larger needles and patt.
Row 1 * K1, p2, k6, p2, rep from * to end.
Row 2 * K2, p6, k2, p1, rep from * to end.
Rows 3 and 4 As rows 1 and 2.
Row 5 * K1, p2, k6, p2, k1, p2, C6F, p2, rep from * to end.
Row 6 As row 2.
Row 7 As row 1.
Row 8 As row 2.
Rows 9 to 16 Rep rows 5 to 8 twice more.
Row 17 * K1, p2, C6F, p2, k1, p2, k6, p2, rep from * to end.
Row 18 As row 2.
Row 19 As row 1.
Row 20 As row 2.
Rows 21 to 28 Rep rows 17 to 20 twice more.
Rows 5 to 28 form the patt and are repeated throughout.
Inc and work into patt 1 st at beg of the next and every foll 6th row until there are 75 sts.
Work straight until back measures 28cm/11in from cast-on edge, ending with at armhole edge.
Shape armhole
Cast/bind off 8 sts at beg of next row.
Dec 1 st at armhole edge on every row until 56 sts rem.
Cont straight in patt until back measures 43cm/17in from cast-on edge, ending with a WS row.
Dec row K2, * [k2 tog] twice, k1, rep from * to last 4 sts, k2 tog, k2. 35 sts.
Cont in moss/seed st until back measures 48cm/19in from cast-on edge, ending at armhole edge.
Shape shoulder
Cast/bind off 9 sts at beg of next and 2 foll alt rows.

Work 1 row.
Cast/bind off rem 8 sts.

RIGHT FRONT

Using smaller needles cast on 41 sts.
Patt row (RS) K1, * p1, k1, rep from * to end.
Rep this row for 2cm/¾in, ending with a RS row.
Inc row Patt 3, * M1, patt 1, M1, patt 2, rep from * to last 2 sts, M1, patt 2. 66 sts.
Change to larger needles and patt.
Row 1 * P2, k6, p2, k1, rep from * to end.
Row 2 * P1, k2, p6, k2, rep from * to end.

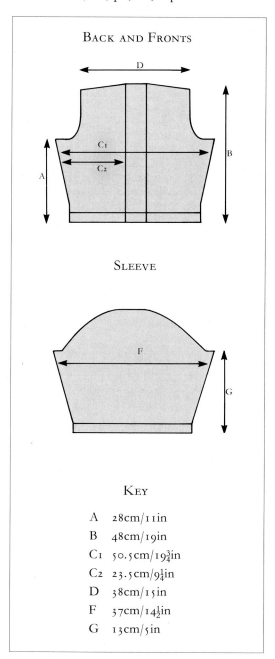

BACK AND FRONTS

SLEEVE

KEY

A   28cm/11in
B   48cm/19in
C1 50.5cm/19¾in
C2 23.5cm/9¼in
D   38cm/15in
F   37cm/14½in
G   13cm/5in

Rows 3 and 4 As rows 1 and 2.
Row 5 * P2, C6F, p2, k1, p2, k6, p2, k1, rep from * to end.
Row 6 As row 2.
The 6 rows just worked set the patt for the right front.
Complete to match left front reversing all the shapings.

SLEEVES
Using smaller needles cast on 61 sts.
Work 2cm/¾in moss/seed st as given for back, ending with a RS row.
Inc row Patt 2, * M1, patt 1, M1, patt 2, rep from * to last 2 sts, M1, patt 2. 100 sts.
Change to larger needles and work in patt as given for back, inc and work into patt 1 st at each end of every 3rd row until there are 118 sts.
Work straight until sleeve measures 13cm/5in from the beginning at cast-on edge, ending with a WS row.

Shape top
Cast/bind off 8 sts at beg of next 2 rows.

Dec 1 st at each end of every row until 28 sts rem.
Cast/bind off.

FRONT BAND
Using smaller needles cast on 11 sts.
Work 4 rows moss/seed st.
Buttonhole row 1 Patt 4, cast/bind off 3, patt to end.
Buttonhole row 2 Patt 4, cast on 3 sts, patt to end.
Cont in patt working 4 more buttonholes 5.5cm/2¼in from cast/bound off edge of previous buttonhole.
Cont in patt until band, when slightly stretched, fits up right front, across back neck and down left front.
Cast/bind off.

FINISHING
Join shoulder seams.
Sew on front band.
Sew in sleeves.
Join side and sleeve seams.
Sew on buttons.

CAMPUS

◆

COMFORTABLE, FLATTERING AND CLASSIC
KNITWEAR HAS ALWAYS SEEMED QUITE THE
MOST NATURAL ATTIRE FOR THE ACADEMIC
ATMOSPHERE OF CAMPUSES AS FAR APART
AS CAMBRIDGE, WELLESLEY OR THE
SORBONNE. LIKE ALL OF MY DESIGNS
THESE EIGHT SWEATERS ARE WORKED IN
NATURAL FIBRES TO MAKE THEM AS LONG
WEARING AND BEAUTIFUL AS ALL THOSE
WONDERFUL GARMENTS OF THE PAST.

Dartmouth

Intrigued by new ways of using cables and Fair Isles,

I find this combination of intarsia and rugged cables

exciting. It is a great sweater for chilly spring

days on bicycle and boat.

———————◆———————

Materials
900g/31¾oz of a medium weight cotton in main colour A
50g/1¾oz each of contrast colours B, C, D, E, F and G
Pair each of 3¼mm (US 3) and 4mm (US 6) knitting needles
Cable needle

Measurements
Actual measurements
Bust 116cm/45½in
Length to shoulders 68.5cm/27in
Sleeve seam 47cm/18½in

Tension/Gauge
24 sts and 28 rows to 10cm/4in measured over patt worked on 4mm (US 6) needles

Please check your tension/gauge carefully and change needle size if necessary

Panel Pattern
Stocking stitch and Cable panels with reversed st st and garter st between are worked over 139 sts as follows:
Row 1 K16, p2, k21, [p2, k16, p2, k21] twice, p2, k16.
Row 2 P16, k2, p10, k1, p10, [k2, p16, k2, p10, k1, p10] twice, k2, p16.
Rows 3 to 10 Rep rows 1 and 2 four times more.
Row 11 K16, p2, k21, [p2, C8B (see page

159), C8F, p2, k21] twice, p2, k16.
Row 12 As row 2.
These 12 rows form the panels and are repeated throughout.

Back
Using smaller needles and A cast on 106 sts.
Rib row 1 (RS) K2, * p2, k2, rep from * to end.
Rib row 2 P2, * k2, p2, rep from * to end.
Rep these 2 rows for 8cm/3¼in ending with rib row 1.
Inc row Rib 5, * M1, rib 3, rep from * to last 5 sts, M1, rib 5. 139 sts.
Change to larger needles.
Work in panel pattern as given above *at the same time* work Fair Isle patt from chart as follows:
Row 1 (RS) Work last 39 sts of row 1, then work 82 sts from chart once, then work first 18 sts of row 1.
Row 2 Work last 18 sts of row 2, then work 82 sts from chart once, then work first 39 sts of row 2.
Cont straight in patt until back measures 42cm/16½in from cast-on edge, ending with a WS row.
Shape armholes
Cast/bind off 3 sts at beg of next 2 rows.
Dec 1 st at each end of the next and every foll alt row until 115 sts rem.
Cont without shaping in patt as set throughout until back measures 68.5cm/27in from

Patt 1 row.
Next row K1, sl 1, k1, psso, patt to end.
Next row Patt to end.
Rep the last 2 rows 3 times more. 37 sts.
Cont straight until front measures same as back to shoulder ending at armhole edge.
Shape shoulder
Cast/bind off 12 sts at beg of next and foll alt row.
Patt 1 row.
Cast/bind off rem 13 sts.

SLEEVES
Using smaller needles and A cast on 50 sts.

cast-on edge, ending with a WS row.
Shape shoulders
Cast/bind off 12 sts at beg of next 4 rows and 13 sts on the foll 2 rows.
Leave rem 41 sts on a spare needle.

FRONT
Work as given for back until front measures 63cm/24¾in from beg ending with a WS row.
Shape neck
Next row Patt 45 sts, turn and leave rem sts on a spare needle.
Cast off 4 sts at beg of next row.
Next row Patt to last 3 sts, k2 tog, k1.
Next row Patt to end.
Rep the last 2 rows 3 times more. 37 sts.
Cont straight until front measures the same as back to shoulder ending at armhole edge.
Shape shoulder
Cast/bind off 12 sts at beg of next and foll alt row.
Patt 1 row.
Cast/bind off rem 13 sts.
With right side facing return to rem sts and slip next 25 sts on to a spare needle, join on yarn, patt to end.

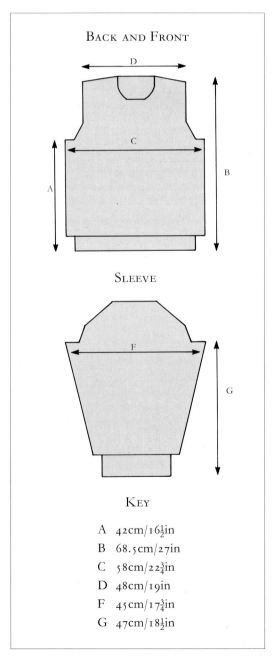

BACK AND FRONT

SLEEVE

KEY

A 42cm/16½in
B 68.5cm/27in
C 58cm/22¾in
D 48cm/19in
F 45cm/17¾in
G 47cm/18½in

Work 10cm/4in rib as given for back, ending with a RS row.

Inc row Rib 3, * M1, rib 2, rep from * to last 3 sts, M1, rib 3. 73 sts.

Change to larger needles and patt.

Row 1 K6, p2, k16, p2, k21, p2, k16, p2, k6.

Row 2 P6, k2, p16, k2, p10, k1, p10, k2, p16, k2, p6.

These 2 rows set the position for the panel patt.

Now cont in panel patt and work from Fair Isle chart as follows:

Row 1 Work last 6 sts of row 65, then work 77 sts from row 65 of chart once.

Row 2 Work last 77 sts of row 66, then work first 6 sts of row 66.

Cont in patt as set, inc 1 st at each end of the next and every foll 4th row until there are 109 sts.

Cont straight in patt until sleeve measures 47cm/18½in from cast-on edge, ending with a WS row.

Shape top

Cast/bind off 5 sts at beg of next 2 rows.

Dec 1 st at each end of the next and 6 foll alt rows.

Work 6 rows straight.

Dec 1 st at each end of every row until 21 sts rem.

Cast/bind off.

Neckband

Join right shoulder seam.

With right side facing using smaller needles and A, pick up and k 22 sts down left side of front neck, 25 sts from centre front, 22 sts up right side of front neck and 41 sts from back neck. 110 sts.

Work 5 rows in rib as given for back.

Cast/bind off in rib.

Finishing

Join left shoulder seam and neckband. Sew in sleeves. Join side and sleeve seams.

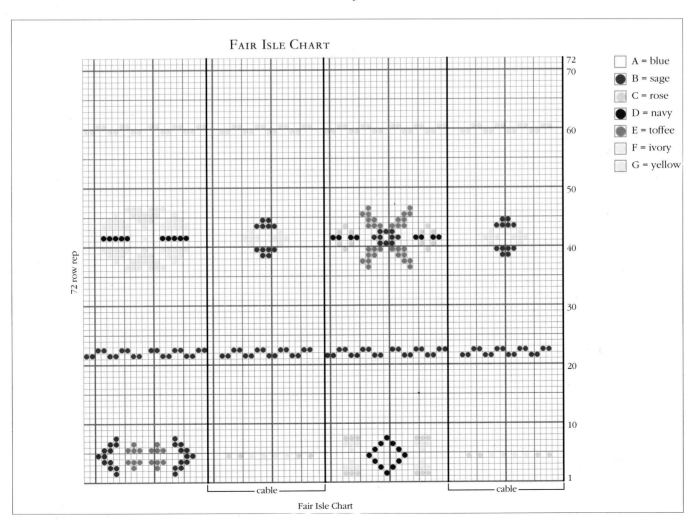

FAIR ISLE CHART

A = blue
B = sage
C = rose
D = navy
E = toffee
F = ivory
G = yellow

72 row rep

cable   cable

Fair Isle Chart

PRINCETON

In this sweater heathery tones of Shetland wool

create a feeling for the moors and heathlands of

northern Britain. It is a lovely warm jacket for

those sporty days outdoors.

———————◆———————

MATERIALS
350g/12½oz of a 4 ply (US sport weight)
Shetland wool in main colour A
50g/1¾oz each of contrast colours B, C, D, E,
F, G, H and I
Pair each of 2¼mm (US 1) and 3¼mm (US 3)
knitting needles
7 buttons

MEASUREMENTS
Actual measurements
Bust 100cm/39½in
Length to shoulders 54.5cm/21½in
Sleeve seam 44.5cm/17½in

TENSION/GAUGE
30 sts and 32 rows to 10cm/4in measured
over st st worked on 3¼mm (US 3) needles

**Please check your tension/gauge carefully
and change needle size if necessary**

BACK
Using smaller needles and A cast on 109 sts.
Rib row 1 (RS) K1, * p1, k1, rep from *
to end.
Rib row 2 P1, * k1, p1, rep from * to end.
Rep these 2 rows for 6cm/2½in ending with
rib row 1.
Inc row Rib 4, * M1, rib 2, M1, rib 3, rep
from * to last 5 sts, M1, rib 5. 150 sts.
Change to larger needles.
Work in st st in patt from chart as foll:

Row 1 (RS) Work last 3 sts of row 1, then
work 24 st patt rep 6 times, then work first 3
sts of row 1.
Row 2 Work last 3 sts of row 2, then work 24
st patt rep 6 times, then work first 3 sts of
row 2.
Cont straight in patt as set until back
measures 30.5cm/12in from cast-on edge,
ending with a WS row.
Shape armholes
Cast/bind off 6 sts at beg of next 2 rows.
Dec 1 st at each end of the next and 5 foll alt
rows. 126 sts.
Cont straight until back measures 54.5cm/
21½in from cast-on edge, ending with a WS
row.
Shape neck
Next row Patt 46 sts, turn and leave rem sts
on a spare needle.
Dec 1 st at neck edge of next 4 rows.
Cast/bind off rem 42 sts.
With right side facing join yarn to rem sts,
cast/bind off next 34 sts, patt to end.
Dec 1 st at neck edge of next 4 rows. Cast/
bind off rem 42 sts.

BREAST POCKET LINING (*make one*)
Using larger needles and A cast on 30 sts.
Work 11cm/4¼in in st st ending with a p row.
Leave sts on a spare needle.

LEFT FRONT
Using smaller needles and A cast on 69 sts.

working in patt foll chart row 2, work last 5 sts of row 2, then work 24 st patt 3 times, then work first 3 sts of row 2.

Keeping 10 edge sts in rib using A as set throughout, cont in patt foll chart from row 3 until front measures 30.5cm/12in from cast-on edge ending at armhole edge and ending with same chart row as back at beg of armhole shaping.

Shape armhole

Cast/bind off 6 sts at beg of next row.

Dec 1 st at armhole edge on the 6 foll alt rows. 78 sts.

Work 1 row, ending with a WS row.

Cont in patt as set until front measures 37cm/14½in from cast-on edge, ending at armhole edge.

Place pocket

Next row (RS) Patt 15 sts, place next 30 sts on a holder, patt across 30 sts of pocket lining, then patt to end.

Cont in patt as set until front measures 49.5cm/19¼in from cast-on edge, ending at neck edge.

Shape neck

Cast/bind off 20 sts at beg of next row then dec 1 st at neck edge on the next 16 rows. 42 sts.

Cont straight in patt until front measures the same as back to shoulder shaping ending at armhole edge. Cast/bind off 42 sts. Fold ribbed hem to WS and sew in place. Sew on buttons, the first to come 1.5cm/½in from cast-on edge, the 2nd 5.5cm/2¼in from cast-on edge, the 7th 1.5cm/½in from beg of neck shaping and the remaining 4 spaced evenly between the 2nd and the 7th.

Work 6cm/2½in rib as given for back ending with a RS row.

Inc row Rib 14, * M1, rib 3, M1, rib 2, rep from * to last 5 sts, M1, rib 5. 90 sts.

Change to larger needles.

Work in st st in patt from chart as foll:

Row 1 (RS) Using A k to last 10 sts, (p1, k1) 5 times for centre front hem.

Row 2 Using A (p1, k1) 5 times, then

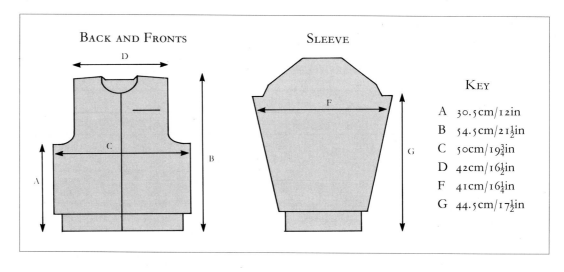

BACK AND FRONTS   SLEEVE

KEY

A   30.5cm/12in
B   54.5cm/21½in
C   50cm/19¾in
D   42cm/16½in
F   41cm/16¼in
G   44.5cm/17½in

RIGHT FRONT

Work to match left front reversing all shapings and colourwork, omitting breast pocket and working buttonholes to correspond with buttons as follows:

Buttonhole row 1 (RS) Patt 3 sts, cast/bind off next 4 sts, patt 6 sts including st already on right-hand needle after cast/bind-off, cast/bind off next 4 sts, patt to end.
Buttonhole row 2 Patt to end, casting on 4 sts over those cast/bound off in last row.

SLEEVES

Using smaller needles and A cast on 63 sts. Work 6cm/2½in rib as given for back, ending with a WS row and increasing 1 st at centre of last row. 64 sts.
Change to larger needles.
Work in st st in patt from chart as foll:
Row 1 Work last 8 sts of chart row 17, then work 24 st patt rep twice, then work first 8 sts of row 17.
Row 2 Work last 8 sts of row 20, then work 24 st patt rep twice, then work first 8 sts of row 20.
Inc and work into patt, 1 st at each end of the next and 7 foll 3rd rows then every foll 4th row until there are 124 sts.
Work straight until sleeve measures 44.5cm/17½in from cast-on edge, ending with a WS row and with same chart row as back at beg of armhole shaping.
Shape top
Cast/bind off 6 sts at beg of next 2 rows.
Dec 1 st at each end of the next and every foll alt row until 44 sts rem.
Cast/bind off.

POCKET TOP

With right side facing using smaller needles and A, increasing 1 st at centre k across sts from holder. 31 sts.
Work 7 rows rib as given for back.
Cast/bind off in rib.

COLLAR

Join shoulder seams. Fold ribbed hem of right front to WS and sew in place.
Using smaller needles and A and with RS facing, beg 1.5cm/½in from centre front and pick up and k 58 sts up right side of front neck, 57 sts from back neck, and 58 sts down

left front neck. 173 sts.
Work 7cm/2¾in in rib as given for back.
Cast/bind off loosely in rib.

FINISHING

Set in sleeves.
Join side and sleeve seams.
Sew pocket and row ends of pocket top in place.

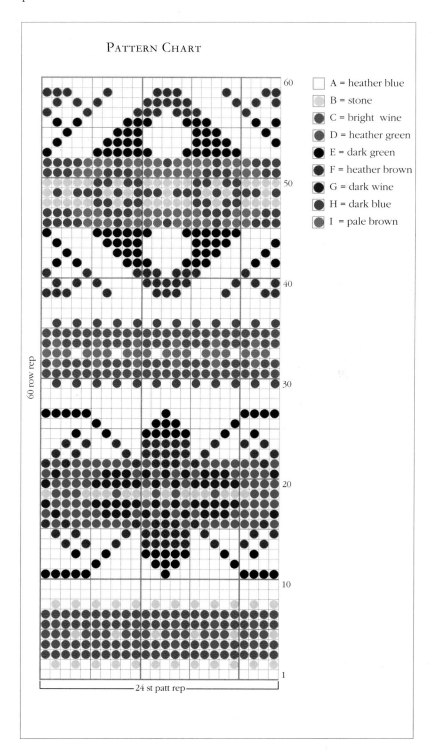

PATTERN CHART

A = heather blue
B = stone
C = bright wine
D = heather green
E = dark green
F = heather brown
G = dark wine
H = dark blue
I = pale brown

60 row rep

24 st patt rep

SOMERVILLE

THE PRETTY SPRING FLOWERS ON THIS COTTON CARDIGAN

ARE GUARANTEED TO CHEER UP ANY LONG DAY SPENT IN THE

LIBRARY. THE NATURAL MOTHER-OF-PEARL BUTTONS

ARE AN OLD FAVOURITE.

———————————◆———————————

MATERIALS
600g/21¼oz of a medium weight cotton in main colour A
50g/1¾oz each of contrast colours B, C, D, E, F, G, H and I
Pair each of 3¼mm (US 3) and 4½mm (US 7) knitting needles
6 buttons

MEASUREMENTS
Actual measurements
Bust 96cm/38in
Length to shoulders 35cm/13½in
Sleeve seam 45cm/17¾in

TENSION/GAUGE
20 sts and 28 rows to 10cm/4in measured over patt worked on 4½mm (US 7) needles

Please check your tension/gauge carefully and change needle size if necessary

NOTE
When working from charts use separate small balls of yarn for each isolated area of colour and twist yarns together at WS of work when changing colour to avoid making a hole.

BACK
Using smaller needles and A cast on 89 sts.
Rib row 1 (RS) K1, * p1, k1, rep from * to end.
Rib row 2 P1, * k1, p1, rep from * to end.

Rep these 2 rows for 6cm/2½in ending with rib row 1.
Inc row Rib 8, * M1, rib 12, rep from * to last 9 sts, M1, rib 9. 96 sts.
Change to larger needles.
Work in patt from chart until row 52 has been worked.
Shape armholes
Cast/bind off 4 sts at beg of next 2 rows. Dec 1 st at each end of the next 4 rows. 80 sts.
Cont straight in patt until row 104 has been worked.
Shape shoulders and neck
Cast/bind off 9 sts at beg of next 2 rows.
Next row Cast/bind off 8 sts, k until there are 8 sts on needle, k2 tog, turn and leave rem sts on a spare needle.
Next row P2 tog, p to end.
Cast/bind off rem 8 sts.
With right side facing, join yarn to rem sts and cast/bind off next 26 sts, k2 tog, patt to end.
Next row Cast/bind off 8 sts, patt to last 2 sts, p2 tog.
Cast/bind off rem 8 sts.

FRONTS
Using smaller needles and A cast on 43 sts.
Rib row 1 (RS) K1, * p1, k1, rep from * to end.
Rib row 2 P1, * k1, p1, rep from * to end.
Rep these 2 rows for 6cm/2½in ending with rib row 1.

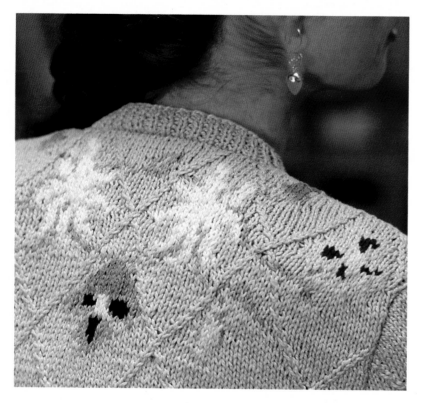

Row 2 K1, * p1, k1, rep from * to end.
Rep these 2 rows until band is long enough when slightly stretched to fit up left front from cast-on edge to top of neckband.
Cast/bind off in rib.
Sew band in place.
Sew on buttons, the first to come 1.5cm/½in from lower edge, the 6th 1.5cm/½in from top edge and the rem 4 spaced evenly between.

BUTTONHOLE BAND

Work to match button band working buttonholes to correspond with buttons as follows:
Buttonhole row Rib 3, yo, k2 tog, rib 2.

FINISHING

Sew buttonhole band in place. Set in sleeves. Join side and sleeve seams.

Inc row Rib 10, * M1, rib 11, rep from * to end. 46 sts.
Change to larger needles and work from chart, shaping sides, neck and shoulder of fronts as shown.
Cast/bind off.

SLEEVES

Using smaller needles and A cast on 39 sts.
Work 8cm/3in rib as given for back, ending with a RS row.
Inc row Rib 4, * M1, rib 5, rep from * to end. 46 sts.
Change to larger needles and work from chart, shaping sides and top of sleeves as shown.
Cast/bind off.

NECKBAND

Join shoulder seams. Using smaller needles and A pick up and k 20 sts up right side of front neck, 33 sts from back neck, and 20 sts down left front neck. 73 sts.
Work 2cm/¾in rib as given for back.
Cast/bind off in rib.

BUTTON BAND

Using smaller needles and A cast on 7 sts.
Row 1 K2, p1, k1, p1, k2.

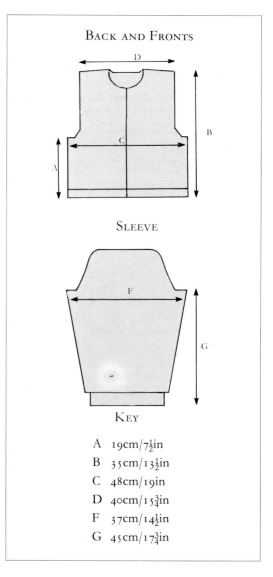

BACK AND FRONTS

SLEEVE

KEY

A 19cm/7½in
B 35cm/13½in
C 48cm/19in
D 40cm/15¾in
F 37cm/14½in
G 45cm/17¾in

SLEEVE

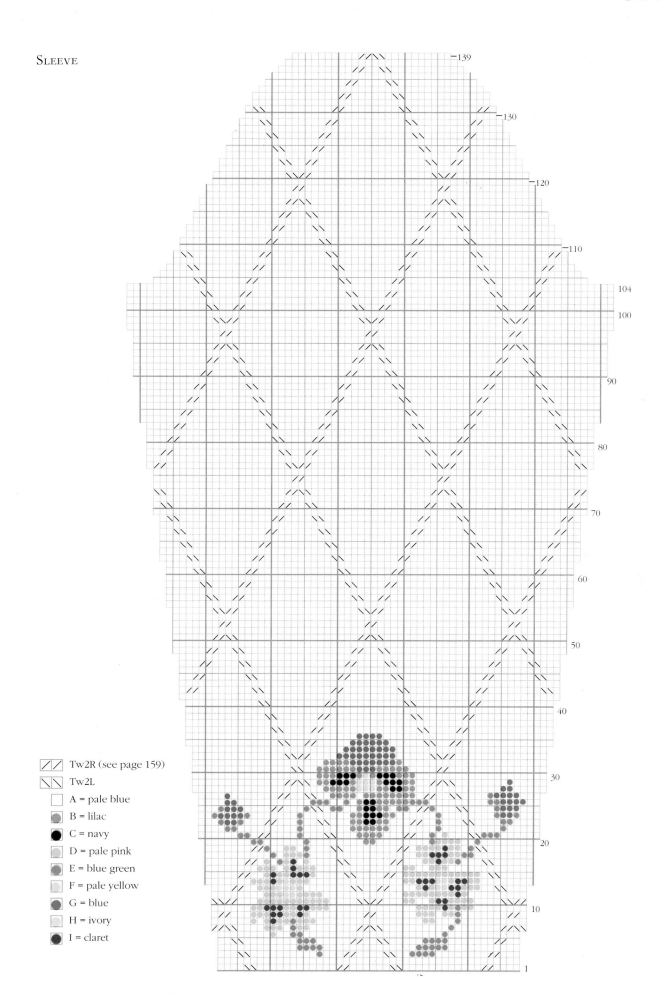

—139

—130

—120

—110

104

100

90

80

70

60

50

40

30

20

10

1

Tw2R (see page 159)
Tw2L
A = pale blue
B = lilac
C = navy
D = pale pink
E = blue green
F = pale yellow
G = blue
H = ivory
I = claret

BACK

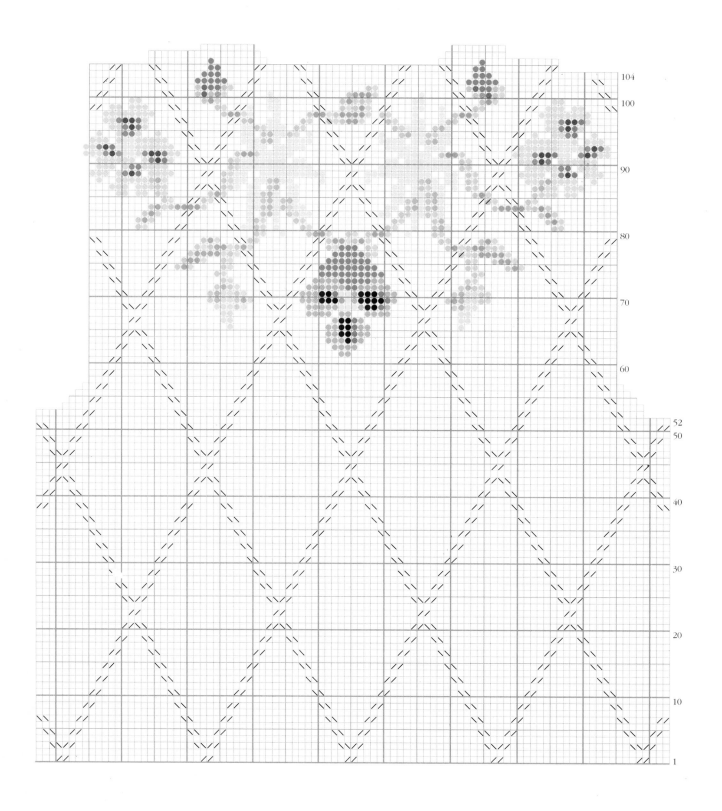

RIGHT FRONT

LEFT FRONT

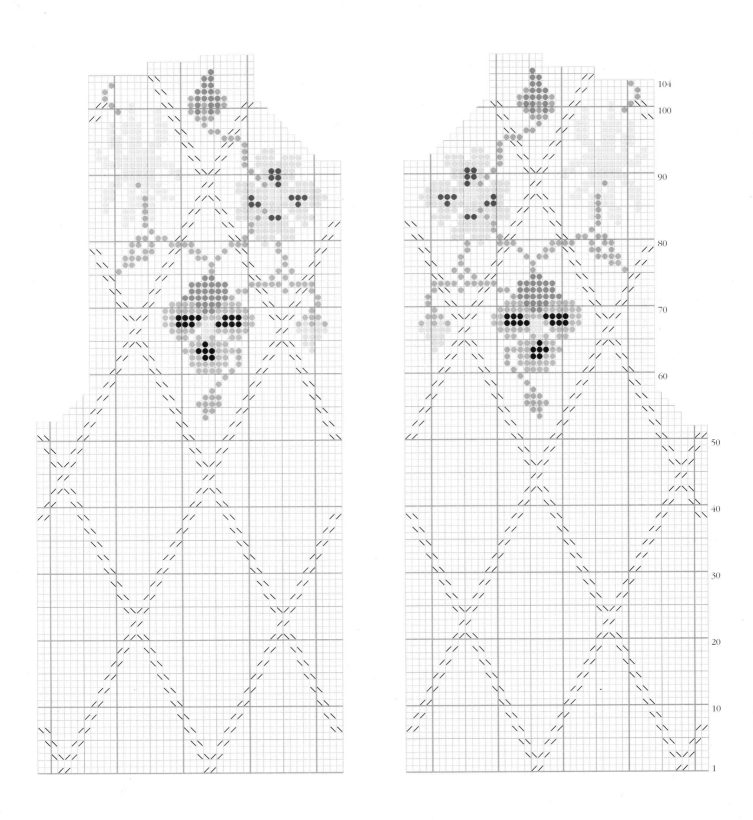

104
100

90

80

70

60

50

40

30

20

10

1

BALLIOL

WITH ITS SOFT, PRETTY SHAPE AND
THE LACY ARAN PATTERN FROM THE
OLD FISHER GANSEYS, THIS IS AN
ECCENTRIC COMBINATION OF THE
CONTEMPORARY AND TRADITIONAL.

———————◆———————

MATERIALS
500g/17¾oz of a lightweight soft cotton
Pair each of 2¼mm (US 1) and 3mm (US 3)
knitting needles
Cable needle
Crochet hook
7 buttons

MEASUREMENTS
Actual measurements
Bust 92cm/36in
Length to shoulders 50cm/19½in
Sleeve seam 47cm/18½in

TENSION/GAUGE
36 sts and 40 rows to 10cm/4in measured
over aran patt worked on 3mm (US 3)
needles

***Please check your tension/gauge carefully
and change needle size if necessary***

Pattern No 1 (worked over 6 sts)
Row 1 P1, k4, p1.
Row 2 K1, p4, k1.
Row 3 P1, C4B (see page 159), p1.
Row 4 K1, p4, k1.
These 4 rows form the patt and are repeated
throughout.

Pattern No 2 (worked over 17 sts)
Row 1 P6, Cr2R, k1, Cr2L, p6.
Row 2 K6, p5, k6.

65

Row 3 P5, Cr2R, k3, Cr2L, p5.
Row 4 K5, p7, k5.
Row 5 P4, [Cr2R] twice, k1, [Cr2L] twice, p4.
Row 6 K4, p9, k4.
Row 7 P3, [Cr2R] twice, k3, [Cr2L] twice, p3.
Row 8 K3, p11, k3.
Row 9 P2, [Cr2R] 3 times, k1, [Cr2L] 3 times, p2
Row 10 K2, p13, k2.
Row 11 P1, [Cr2R] 3 times, k3, [Cr2L] 3 times, p1.
Row 12 K1, p15, k1.
Row 13 P1, k1, [Cr2R] 3 times, k1, [Cr2L] 3 times, k1, p1.
Row 14 As row 12.
Row 15 P1, Cr2L, [Cr2R] twice, k3, [Cr2L] twice, Cr2R, p1.
Row 16 As row 10.
Row 17 P2, Cr2L, [Cr2R] twice, k1, [Cr2L] twice, Cr2R, p2.
Row 18 As row 8.
Row 19 P3, Cr2L, Cr2R, k3, Cr2L, Cr2R, p3.
Row 20 As row 6.
Row 21 P4, Cr2L, Cr2R, k1, Cr2L, Cr2R, p4.
Row 22 As row 4.
Row 23 P5, Cr2L, k3, Cr2R, p5.
Row 24 As row 2.
Row 25 P6, Cr2L, k1, Cr2R, p6.
Row 26 K7, p3, k7.
Rep these 26 rows to form the patt.

Pattern No 3 (worked over 39 sts)
Row 1 * P1, k3, p7, k3, p1*, k4, p1, k4, rep from * to * once more.
Row 2 * K1, p5, sl 1, p2 tog, psso, p5, k1 *, p4, k1, p4, rep from * to * once more.
Row 3 * P1, k1, yo, k2, p5, k2, yo, k1, p1 *, k4, p1, k4, rep from * to * once more.
Row 4 As row 2.
Row 5 * P1, k2, yo, k2, p3, k2, yo, k2, p1 *, k4, p1, k4, rep from * to * once more.
Row 6 As row 2.
Row 7 * P1, k3, yo, k5, yo, k3, p1 *, C4F, p1, C4F, rep from * to * once more.
Row 8 * K1, p13, k1*, p4, k1, p4, rep from * to * once more.
Row 9 * P5, k2, yo, k1, yo, k2, p5 *, k4, p1, k4, rep from * to * once more.

Row 10 K1, p15, [k1, p4] twice, k1, p15, k1.
Row 11 * P3, p2 tog, k2, yo, k3, yo, k2, p2 tog, p3 *, k4, p1, k4, rep from * to * once more.
Row 12 As row 10.
Row 13 * P2, p2 tog, k2, yo, k5, yo, k2, p2 tog, p2 *, k4, p1, k4, rep from * to * once more.
Row 14 As row 10.
Row 15 * P1, p2 tog, k2, p7, k2, p2 tog, p1 *, k4, p1, k4, rep from * to * once more.
Row 16 As row 2.

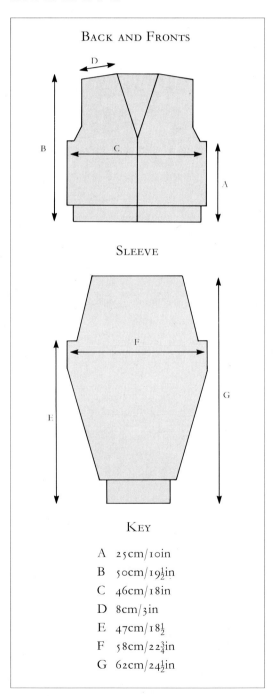

BACK AND FRONTS

SLEEVE

KEY

A 25cm/10in
B 50cm/19½in
C 46cm/18in
D 8cm/3in
E 47cm/18½
F 58cm/22¾in
G 62cm/24½in

Row 17 * P1, k1, yo, k2, p5, k2, yo, k1, p1*, k4, p1, k4, rep from * to * once more.

Row 18 As row 2.

Row 19 * P1, k2, yo, k2, p3, k2, yo, k2, p1 *, k4, p1, k4, rep from * to * once more.

Row 20 As row 2.

Row 21 * P1, k3, yo, k5, yo, k3. p1 *, C4F, p1, C4F, rep from * to * once more.

Row 22 As row 8.

Rows 9 to 22 form the patt and are repeated throughout.

BACK

Using smaller needles cast on 105 sts.

Rib row 1 (RS) * K4, k1 tbl, p2, rep from * to end.

Rib row 2 * K2, p1 tbl, p4, rep from * to end.

Rib row 3 * K4, Cr2Lp (see page 159), p1, rep from * to end.

Rib row 4 * K1, p1 tbl, k1, p4, rep from * to end.

Rib row 5 * K4, p1, Cr2Lp, rep from * to end.

Rib row 6 * P1 tbl, k2, p4, rep from * to end.

Rib row 7 * K4, p1, Cr2Rp, rep from * to end.

Rib row 8 * K1, p1 tbl, k1, p4, rep from * to end.

Rib row 9 * K4, Cr2Rp, p1, rep from * to end.

Rep rows 2 to 9 for 5.5cm/2¼in ending with a RS row.

Inc row Patt 3, M1, patt 2, * M1, patt 7, rep from * ending last rep patt 2. 121 sts.

Change to larger needles.

Work in chevron patt as follows:

Row 1 K1, * yo, sl 1, k1, psso, k10, k2 tog, yo, k1, yo, sl 1, k1, psso, k10, k2 tog, yo, k1, rep from * to end.

Row 2 and every alt row P to end.

Row 3 K2, * yo, sl 1, k1, psso, k8, k2 tog, yo, k3, rep from * ending last rep k2.

Row 5 K3, * yo, sl 1, k1, psso, k6, k2 tog, yo, k5, rep from * ending last rep k3.

Row 7 K4, * yo, sl 1, k1, psso, k4, k2 tog, yo, k7, rep from * ending last rep k4.

Row 9 K5, * yo, sl 1, k1, psso, k2, k2 tog, yo, k9, rep from * ending last rep k5.

Rib 10 P5, M1p, p3, * M1p, p3, M1p, p4, rep from * ending last rep p5. 154 sts.

Now work in aran patt as follows:

Row 1 [K1, p1] 4 times, work row 1 of pattern No 1 over next 6 sts, k1, work row 1 of pattern No 1 over next 6 sts, work row 1 of pattern No 2 over next 17 sts, work row 1 of pattern No 3 twice over next 78 sts, work row 1 of pattern No 2 over next 17 sts, work row 1 of pattern No 1 over next 6 sts, k1, work row 1 of pattern No 1 over next 6 sts, [k1, p1] 4 times.

Row 2 [P1, k1] 4 times, work row 2 of pattern No 1 over next 6 sts, p1, work row 2 of pattern No 1 over next 6 sts, work row 2 of pattern No 2 over next 17 sts, work row 2 of pattern No 3 twice over next 78 sts, work row 2 of pattern No 2 over next 17 sts, work row 2 of pattern No 1 over next 6 sts, p1, work row 2 of pattern No 1 over next 6 sts, [p1, k1] 4 times.

Keeping 8sts at each end in moss/seed st cont in patt as set until back measures 25cm/10in from cast-on edge, ending with a WS row.

Shape armholes

Cast/bind off 10 sts beg of next 2 rows. Dec 1 st at each end of the next and every foll alt row until 108 sts rem.

Cont straight until back measures 50cm/19½in from cast-on edge, ending with a WS row.

Shape shoulders

Cast/bind off 9sts at beg of next 6 rows. Cast/bind off rem 54 sts.

LEFT FRONT

Using smaller needles cast on 56 sts.

Work in rib patt as given for back for 5.5cm/2¼in ending with a RS row.

Inc row Patt 12, * M1, patt 7, rep from * 3 times more, M1, patt to end. 61 sts.

Change to larger needles.

Work 9 rows in chevron patt as given for back.

Row 10 P2 * M1p, p3, rep from * ending last rep p2. 81 sts.

Now work in aran patt as follows:

Row 1 [K1, p1] 4 times, work row 1 of pattern No 1 over next 6 sts, k1, work row 1 of pattern No 1 over next 6 sts, work row 1 of pattern No 2 over next 17 sts, work row 1 of pattern No 3 over next 39 sts, [k1, p1] twice.

Row 2 [P1, k1] twice, work row 2 of pattern No 3 over next 39 sts, work row 2 of pattern

No 2 over next 17 sts, work row 2 of pattern No 1 over next 6 sts, p1, work row 2 of pattern No 1 over next 6 sts, [p1, k1] 4 times.

Keeping 8 sts at armhole edge and 4 sts at front edge in moss/seed st cont in patt as set until front measures 25cm/10in from cast-on edge, ending at armhole edge.

Shape armhole and front neck

Cast/bind off 10 sts at beg of next row. Dec 1 st at armhole edge on every RS row 13 times then keep armhole edge straight *at the same time* dec 1 st at neck edge on next and every foll 3rd row until 27 sts rem.

Work straight until front measures 50cm/19½in from cast-on edge, ending at armhole edge.

Shape shoulder

Cast/bind off 9 sts at beg of next and foll alt row. Work 1 row.

Cast/bind off rem 9 sts.

RIGHT FRONT

Work as given for left front reversing all shapings.

SLEEVES

Using smaller needles cast on 56 sts.

Work in rib patt as given for back for 8cm/3in ending with a RS row.

Inc row Patt 2, [M1, patt 1, M1, patt 2] 17 times, M1, patt 3. 91 sts.

Change to larger needles.

Work in 9 rows in chevron patt as given for back.

Row 10 P3 * M1p, p3, M1, p2, rep from * to last 3 sts, M1, p3. 126 sts.

Now work in aran patt as follows:

Row 1 K1, work row 1 of pattern No 1 over next 6 sts, work row 1 of pattern No 2 over next 17 sts, work row 1 of pattern No 3 twice over next 78 sts, work row 1 of pattern No 2 over next 17 sts, work row 1 of pattern No 1 over next 6 sts, k1.

Row 2 P1, work row 2 of pattern No 1 over next 6 sts, work row 2 of pattern No 2 over next 17 sts, work row 2 of pattern No 3 twice over next 78 sts, work row 2 of pattern No 2 over next 17 sts, work row 2 of pattern No 1 over next 6 sts, p1.

Inc 1 st at each end of the next and every foll 4th row until there are 190 sts, working the first 6 sts increased at each end in patt No 1 and the remainder of sts increased in moss/seed st.

Cont straight until sleeve measures 47cm/18½in from cast-on edge ending with a WS row.

Shape sleeve top

Cast/bind off 10 sts at beg of next 2 rows.

Dec 1 st at each end of the next and every foll 6th row until 150 sts rem. Work 3 rows in patt.

Next row * Work 3 sts tog, rep from * to end. 50 sts.

Cast/bind off.

FRONT BAND

Join shoulder seams for 8cm/3in from armhole edge. Sew buttons to left front in centre of moss/seed st band, the first 1.5cm/½in from lower edge, the 7th level with first row of neck shaping and the remaining 5 buttons spaced evenly between.

Taking care not to stetch the work, join on yarn to cast-on edge of right front, work in dc/sc (see page 159) up right front, across back neck and down left front, turn and work 1 more row in dc/sc.

Button loop row Work in dc/sc to position on right front corresponding to first button on left front, then work 6ch, 1 dc/sc in same place as last dc/sc, * work in dc/sc to position corresponding to next button, 6ch, 1 dc/sc in same place as last dc/sc, rep from * 5 times more, work in dc/sc to end of row, so ending at lower edge of left front. Fasten off.

FINISHING

Mark a point 6cm/2½in down from shoulder seam on back and fronts. With cast/bound off edge of sleeve head between markers, sew in sleeves. Join side and sleeve seams.

S O R B O N N E

THIS IS THE ULTIMATE CHIC SWEATER. ITS CLASSIC LINES

MAKE IT SO EASY TO DRESS UP OR DOWN FOR ANY OCCASION. TRY

KNITTING IT IN A SILK OR WOOL-AND-SILK YARN TO FEEL

EXTRA LUXURIOUS.

---◆---

MATERIALS
325g/11½oz of a 4 ply (US sport weight)
botany wool
Pair each of 2¼mm (US 1) and 3¼mm (US 3)
knitting needles
1 spare 3¼mm (US 3) needle
Cable needle
3 buttons

MEASUREMENTS
Actual measurements
Bust 96cm/38in
Length to shoulders 50.5cm/20in
Sleeve seam 44.5cm/17½in

TENSION/GAUGE
30 sts and 42 rows to 10cm/4in measured
over patt worked on 3¼mm (US 3) needles

***Please check your tension/gauge carefully
and change needle size if necessary***

BACK
Using smaller needles cast on 130 sts.
Rib row 1 (RS) K2, * p2, k2, rep from * to
end.
Rib row 2 P2, * k2, p2, rep from * to end.
Rep these 2 rows for 13cm/5in ending with
rib row 1.
Inc row Rib 6, * M1, rib 9, rep from * to last
7 sts, M1, rib 7. 144 sts.
Change to larger needles. Work in patt from
chart until row 78 has been worked.

Shape armholes
Cast/bind off 5 sts at beg of next 2 rows.
Dec 1 st at each end of the next 4 rows and
the 4 foll alt rows. 118 sts.
Cont straight from chart until row 152 has
been worked.
** Next row (RS) With larger needles patt
26 sts from chart, then with smaller needles
[k1, p1] 33 times, then with larger needles
patt 26 sts from chart.
Next row With larger needles patt 26 sts
from chart, then with smaller needles [p1,
k1] 33 times, then with larger needles patt 26
sts from chart.
Repeat these 2 rows 5 times more.
Shape neck
With larger needles patt 26 sts, then with
smaller needles moss/seed st 11 sts, turn and
leave rem sts on a spare needle.
Cont straight on these sts keeping 11 neck
edge sts in moss/seed st until row 176 has
been worked.
Shape shoulder
Keeping continuity of patt, cast/bind off 9
sts at beg of next and foll alt row.
Work 1 row.
Cast/bind off rem 19 sts.
With right side facing, using smaller needles
join yarn to rem sts and cast/bind off 44 sts,
work in moss/seed st across next 10 sts, then
using larger needles, patt to end. 37 sts.
Cont straight on these sts until row 177 has
been worked.

Shape shoulder

Keeping continuity of patt, cast/bind off 9 sts at beg of next row and foll alt row.
Cast/bind off rem 19 sts.

FRONT

Work as given for back until row. 114 has been worked.

Shape front neck and opening

Next row Patt 37 sts, turn and leave rem sts on a spare needle.

Next row Using smaller needles cast on 11 sts, work k1, [p1, k1] 5 times across these 11 sts, then using larger needles, patt to end. 48 sts.

Work straight in patt as set until row 138 has been worked.

Next row Using larger needle, patt 26 sts, using smaller needles [p1, k1] 11 times.

Work straight in patt as set until row 149 has been worked.

Next row Cast/bind off 11 sts, patt to end.

Cont straight on these sts until row 176 has been worked.

Shape shoulder

Keeping continuity of patt, cast/bind off 9 sts at beg of next and foll alt row.

Work 1 row. Cast/bind off rem 19 sts.

With right side facing return to sts on spare needle, using smaller needle, p1, [k1, p1] 5 times, using larger needles, patt to end. 81 sts.

Work 7 rows in patt as set.

Buttonhole row 1 (RS) Using smaller needles moss/seed st 4, cast/bind off 3 sts, moss/seed st next 3 sts, using larger needles patt to end.

Buttonhole row 2 Patt to end, casting on 3

sts over those cast/bound off in last row.

Work 10 rows in patt as set, then rep the 2 buttonhole rows.

Work 2 more rows in patt, so ending with row 138.

Next row (RS) Using smaller needles, p1, [k1, p1] 27 times, using larger needles patt to end.

Work 7 more rows in patt as set.

Buttonhole row 1 (RS) Using smaller needles moss/seed st 4, cast/bind off 3 sts, moss/seed st next 47 sts, using larger needles patt to end.

Buttonhole row 2 Patt to end, casting on 3 sts over those cast/bound off in previous row.

Work 2 more rows in patt as set.

Next row Cast/bind off 44 sts, patt to end. 37 sts.

Cont straight on these sts until row 177 has been worked.

Shape shoulder

Keeping continuity of patt, cast/bind off 9 sts at beg of next row and foll alt row.
Cast/bind off rem 19 sts.

SLEEVES

Using smaller needles cast on 62 sts.

Work 9cm/3½in rib as given for back, ending with a RS row.

Inc row Rib 3, * M1, rib 5, rep from * to last 4 sts, M1, rib 4. 74 sts.

Change to larger needles and work from chart, shaping sides of sleeves as shown.

FINISHING

Join shoulder seams. Set in sleeves. Join side and sleeve seams. Sew on buttons.

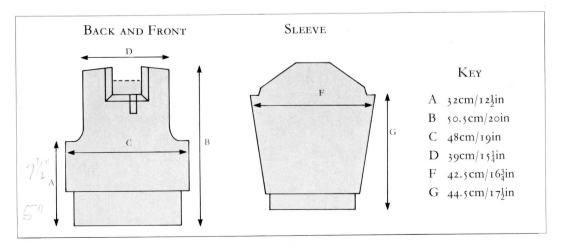

	BACK AND FRONT	SLEEVE	KEY

KEY
A   32cm/12½in
B   50.5cm/20in
C   48cm/19in
D   39cm/15¼in
F   42.5cm/16¾in
G   44.5cm/17½in

SLEEVE

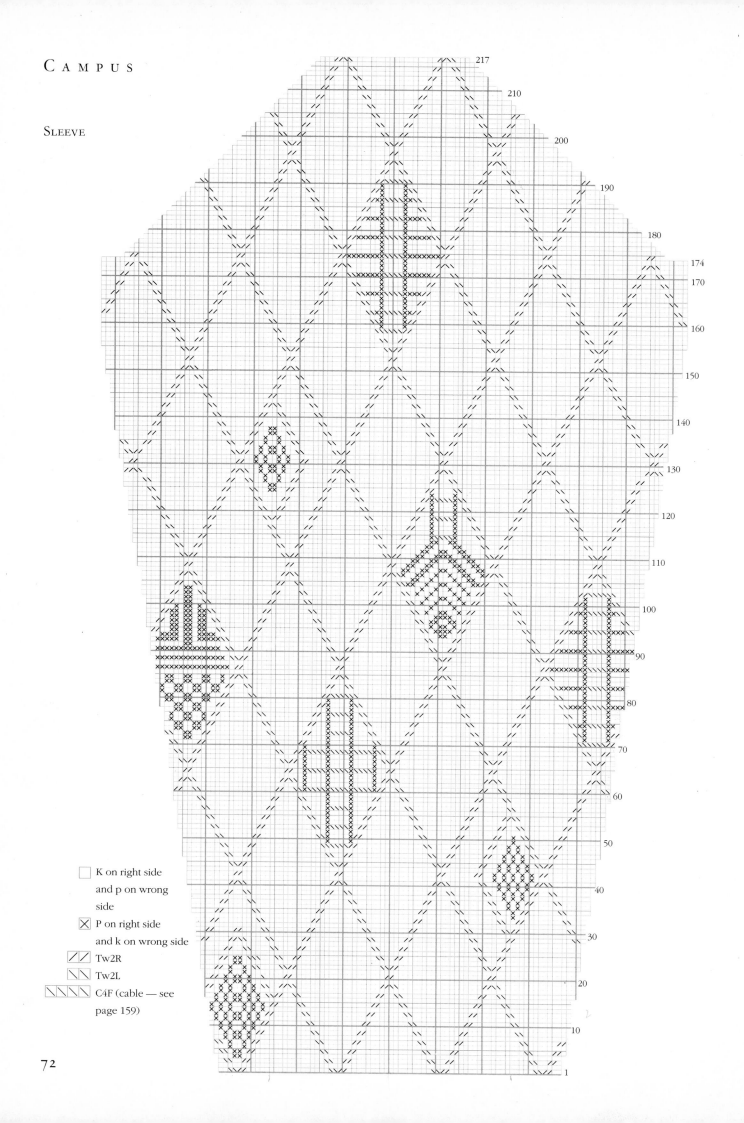

K on right side
and p on wrong
side

P on right side
and k on wrong side

Tw2R

Tw2L

C4F (cable — see
page 159)

217
210
200
190
180
174
170
160
150
140
130
120
110
100
90
80
70
60
50
40
30
20
10
1

BACK AND FRONT

176
170
160
150
140
130
120
114*
110
100
90
80
78
70
60
50
40
30
20
10
1

* Omit cable in centre motif when
working front

Wellesley

Long and loose and knitted in soft, floppy cotton, this sweater is both comfortable and flattering. The dusty colours remind me of a misty autumn morning.

———————◆———————

Materials
350g/12½oz of a lightweight soft cotton in main colour A
50g/1¾oz each of contrast colours B, C, D, E, F and G
Pair each of 2¼mm (US 1) and 3¼mm (US 3) knitting needles
Set of 2¼mm (US 1) double pointed knitting needles

Measurements
Actual measurements
Bust 105cm/41½in
Length to shoulders 62cm/24½in
Sleeve seam 20cm/8in

Tension/Gauge
32 sts and 38 rows to 10cm/4in measured over patt worked on 3¼mm (US 3) needles

Please check your tension/gauge carefully and change needle size if necessary

Note
When working from charts use separate small balls of yarn for each isolated area of colour and twist yarns together at WS of work when changing colour to avoid making a hole.

Back
Using smaller needles and A cast on 114 sts.
Rib row 1 (RS) K2, * p2, k2, rep from * to end of row.

Rib row 2 P2, * k2, p2, rep from * to end.
Rep these 2 rows for 1.5cm/½in ending with rib row 1.
Inc row Rib 4, * M1, rib 2, rep from * to last 4 sts, M1, rib 4. 168 sts.
Change to larger needles. K1 row, p1 row.
Work in patt from chart as follows:
Row 3 (RS) Work last 4 sts of row 3, then work 32 st patt rep 5 times, then work first 4 sts of row 3.
Row 4 Work last 4 sts of row 4, then work 32 st patt rep 5 times, then work first 4 sts of row 4.
Cont in patt as set until back measures 38cm/15in from cast-on edge, ending with a WS row.
Shape armholes
Keeping continuity of patt, cast/bind off 8 sts at beg of next 2 rows. 152 sts.
Cont straight until back measures 62cm/24½in from cast-on edge, ending with a WS row.
Shape shoulders
Cast/bind off 23 sts at beg of next 4 rows.
Leave the rem 60 sts on a spare needle.

Front
Work as given for back until front measures 58.5cm/23in from beg ending with a WS row.
Shape neck
Next row Patt 61 sts, turn and leave rem sts on a spare needle.

Cont in patt as set until row 87 has been worked, then cont in A only until sleeve measures 20cm/8in from cast-on edge, ending with a p row.
Cast/bind off.

NECKBAND
Join shoulder seams.
Using 3 of the double pointed needles and A, starting at left shoulder, pick up and k 17 sts evenly down left side of front neck, k across 30 sts from front neck holder, pick up and k 17 sts up right side of front neck, k across 60 sts from back neck holder. 124 sts.
Work in rounds of k2, p2 rib for 2cm/¾in.
Cast/bind off in rib.

FINISHING
Set in sleeves. Join side and sleeve seams.

** Dec 1 st at neck edge on the next 15 rows. 46 sts.
Cont straight until front measures the same as back to shoulder ending at armhole edge.
Shape shoulder
Cast/bind off 23 sts at beg of next row.
Work 1 row.
Cast/bind off rem 23 sts. **
With right side facing return to rem sts and slip next 30 sts on to a spare needle, join on yarn, patt to end.
Complete to match first side from ** to **.

SLEEVES
Using smaller needles and A cast on 130 sts.
Work 2cm/¾in rib as given for back, ending with a RS row.
Inc row Rib 6, * M1, rib 7, rep from * to last 5 sts, M1, rib 5. 148 sts.
Change to larger needles and work from chart as follows:
Row 1 Work last 10 sts of row 45 then work 32 st patt rep 4 times, then work first 10 sts of row 45.
Row 2 Work last 10 sts of row 46, then work 32 st patt rep 4 times, then work first 10 sts of row 46.

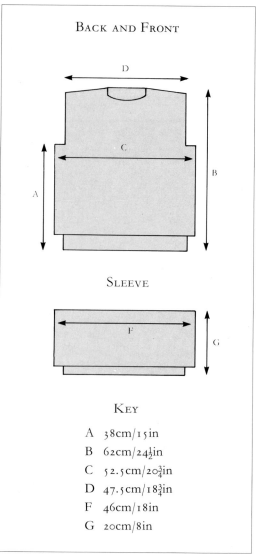

BACK AND FRONT

SLEEVE

KEY

A   38cm/15in
B   62cm/24½in
C   52.5cm/20¾in
D   47.5cm/18¾in
F   46cm/18in
G   20cm/8in

PATTERN CHART

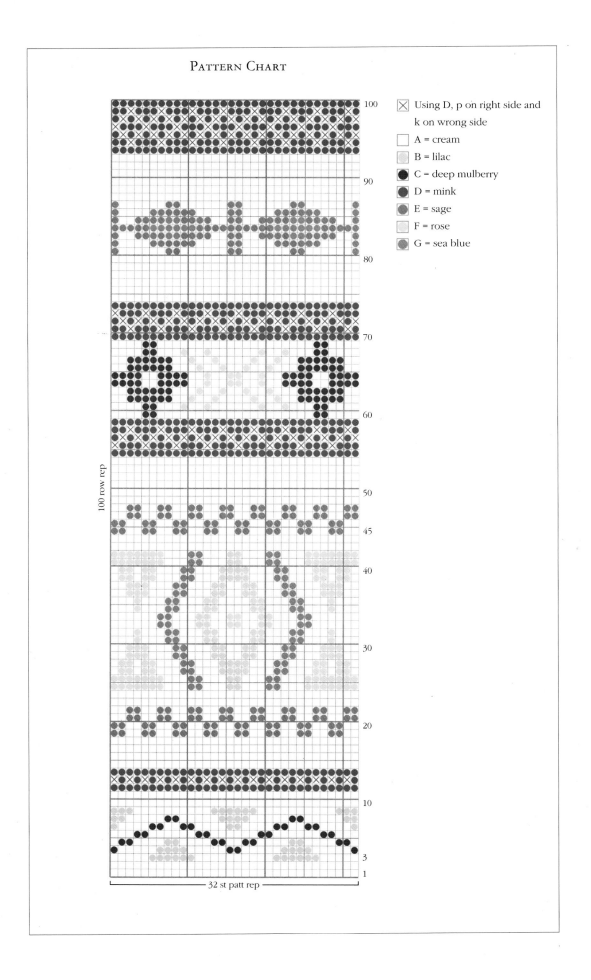

Using D, p on right side and
k on wrong side

A = cream

B = lilac

C = deep mulberry

D = mink

E = sage

F = rose

G = sea blue

100 row rep

32 st patt rep

R A D C L I F F E

THIS JACKET WAS INSPIRED BY THOSE WITH WONDERFUL PEWTER

BUTTONS WORN BY THE TYROLEANS. BUT DON'T YOU THINK THAT

THERE IS ALSO MORE THAN A HINT OF CHANEL IN THERE TOO?

———————◆———————

MATERIALS
700g/24¾oz of a 4 ply (US sport weight)
Shetland wool in main colour A
50g/1¾oz of contrast colour B
Pair each of 3mm (US 2) and 3¾mm (US 5)
knitting needles
Cable needle
6 buttons

MEASUREMENTS
Actual measurements
Bust 106cm/42in
Length to shoulders 53cm/21in
Sleeve seam 46cm/18in

TENSION/GAUGE
20 sts and 32 rows to 10cm/4in measured
over patt worked on 3¾mm (US 5) needles
with yarn used double

***Please check your tension/gauge carefully
and change needle size if necessary***

NOTE
Use yarn double throughout.

Pattern No 1 (worked over 10 sts)
Row 1 P2, [k2, p2] twice.
Row 2 K2, [p2, k2] twice.
Row 3 P2, slip the next 4 sts on to a cable
needle and leave at the front of the work, k2,
then place the p2 sts back on to left hand
needle, take the cable needle to the back of

the work, p2, then k2 from cable needle, p2.
Row 4 As row 2.
Rows 5 to 10 Rep rows 1 and 2 three times.
These 10 rows form the patt and are repeated
throughout.

Pattern No 2 (worked over 12 sts)
Row 1 P2, [k1 tbl] twice, k4, [k1 tbl] twice,
p2.
Row 2 K2, [p1 tbl] twice, p4, [p1 tbl] twice,
k2.
Rows 3 and 4 As rows 1 and 2.
Row 5 P2, [k1 tbl] twice, C4B (see page 159),
[k1 tbl] twice, p2.
Row 6 As row 1.
Rows 7 and 8 As rows 1 and 2.
Row 9 P2, slip the next 4 sts on to a cable
needle and leave at the back of the work, k2,
then k the first 2 sts from the cable needle,
bring the cable needle to the front of the
work, k2, then k2 from the cable needle,
ending with p2.
Row 10 As row 2.
These 10 rows form the patt and are repeated
throughout.

Pattern No 3 (worked over 19 sts)
Row 1 P7, Tw2L, k1, Tw2R, p7.
Row 2 K8, p3, k8.
Row 3 P7, Tw2R, k1, Tw2L, p7.
Row 4 K7, p5, k7.
Row 5 P6, Tw2R, k3, Tw2L, p6.
Row 6 K6, p7, k6.

Row 7 P5, [Tw2R] twice, k1, [Tw2L] twice, p5.

Row 8 K5, p9, k5.

Row 9 P4, [Tw2R] twice, k3, [Tw2L] twice, p4.

Row 10 K4, p11, k4.

Row 11 P3, [Tw2R] 3 times, k1, [Tw2L] 3 times, p3.

Row 12 K3, p13, k3.

Row 13 P2, [Tw2R] 3 times, k3, [Tw2L] 3 times, p2.

Row 14 K2, p15, k2.

Row 15 P2, k1, [Tw2R] 3 times, k1, [Tw2L] 3 times, k1, p2.

Row 16 As row 14.

Row 17 P2, Tw2L, [Tw2R] twice, k3, [Tw2L] twice, Tw2R, p2.

Row 18 As row 12.

Row 19 P3, Tw2L, [Tw2R] twice, k1, [Tw2L] twice, Tw2R, p3.

Row 20 As row 10.

Row 21 P4, Tw2L, Tw2R, k3, Tw2L, Tw2R, p4.

Row 22 As row 8.

Row 23 P5, Tw2L, Tw2R, k1, Tw2L, Tw2R, p5.

Row 24 As row 6.

Row 25 P6, Tw2L, k3, Tw2R, p6.

Row 26 As row 4.

Rep these 26 rows to form the patt.

BACK

Using larger needles and A used double cast on 106 sts.

Foundation row 1 (WS) P to end.

Row 1 For moss/seed st [k1, p1] 6 times, work row 1 of pattern No 2 over next 12 sts, work row 1 of pattern No 1 over next 10 sts, work row 1 of pattern No 3 twice over next 38 sts, work row 1 of pattern No 1 over next 10 sts, work row 1 of pattern No 2 over next 12 sts, for moss/seed st [p1, k1] 6 times.

Row 2 For moss/seed st [k1, p1] 6 times, work row 2 of pattern No 2 over next 12 sts, work row 2 of pattern No 1 over next 10 sts, work row 2 of pattern No 3 twice over next 38 sts, work row 2 of pattern No 1 over next 10 sts, work row 2 of pattern No 2 over next 12 sts, for moss/seed st [p1, k1] 6 times.

Cont straight in patt as set until back measures 32cm/12½in from cast-on edge, ending with a WS row.

Shape armholes

Cast/bind off 5 sts at beg of next 2 rows.

Dec 1 st at each end of the next and 2 foll alt rows. 90 sts.

Cont straight in patt until back measures 53cm/21in from cast-on edge, ending with a WS row.

Shape shoulders

Cast/bind off 10 sts at beg of next 4 rows and 11 sts at beg of foll 2 alt rows.

Cast/bind off rem 28 sts.

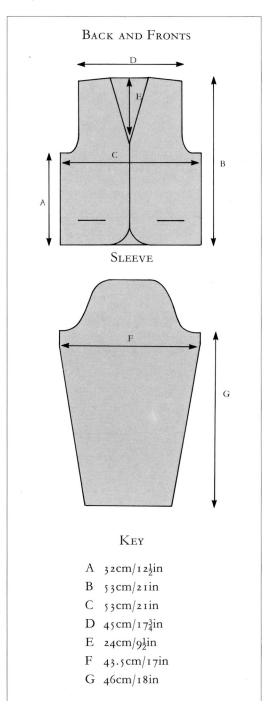

BACK AND FRONTS

SLEEVE

KEY

A   32cm/12½in
B   53cm/21in
C   53cm/21in
D   45cm/17¾in
E   24cm/9½in
F   43.5cm/17in
G   46cm/18in

POCKET LININGS (make 2)
Using smaller needles and A used double
cast on 26 sts.
Work 10cm/4in in st st ending with a k row.
Leave these sts on a holder.

LEFT FRONT
Using larger needles and A used double cast
on 43 sts.
Foundation row 1 (WS) P to end.
Row 1 For moss/seed st [k1, p1] 6 times,
work row 1 of pattern No 2 over next 12 sts,
work row 1 of pattern No 1 over next 10 sts,
work first 8 sts of row 1 of pattern No 3 over
next 8 sts, inc in last st. 44 sts.
Row 2 Inc in first st, work last 9 sts of row 2
of pattern No 3 over next 9 sts, work row 2
of pattern No 1 over next 10 sts, work row 2
of pattern No 2 over next 12 sts, for moss/
seed st [p1, k1] 6 times. 45 sts.
Row 3 For moss/seed st [k1, p1] 6 times,
work row 3 of pattern No 2 over next 12 sts,
work row 3 of pattern No 1 over next 10 sts,
work first 10 sts of row 3 of pattern No 3
over next 10 sts, inc in last st. 46 sts.
Row 4 Inc in first st, work last 11 sts of row 4
of pattern No 3 over next 11 sts, work row 4
of pattern No 1 over next 10 sts, work row 4
of pattern No 2 over next 12 sts, for moss/
seed st [p1, k1] 6 times. 47 sts.
Working the next 8 increased sts into patt
No 3 and the last 5 sts into moss/seed st patt,
inc and work into patt 1 st at front edge on
the next 2 rows then on 5 foll alt rows, then
on 4 foll 3rd rows. 58 sts.
Cont in patt as set until front measures 13cm/
5in from cast-on edge, ending with a WS
row.
Place pocket
Next row Patt 10 sts, cast/bind off next 26
sts, then patt to end.
Next row Patt 22 sts, p across 26 sts of
pocket lining, patt to end.
Cont in patt as set until front measures 29cm/
11½in from cast-on edge ending at neck edge.
Cast/bind off 2 sts at beg of next row, then
dec 1 st on every foll 4th row 17 times *at the
same time* when front measures 32cm/12½in
from cast-on edge ending at armhole edge,
shape armhole by casting/binding off 5 sts at
the beg of next row, then dec 1 st on the foll 3
alt rows.

Shape front neck and armhole
Cont straight in patt until front measures the
same as back to shoulder shaping ending at
armhole edge.
Shape shoulder
Cast/bind off 10 sts at beg of next and foll alt
row. Work 1 row.
Cast/bind off rem 11 sts.
Sew on 4 buttons, the first to come at end of
shaping on lower edge, the 4th to come level
with beg of neck shaping and the remaining
2 spaced evenly between.

RIGHT FRONT
Work to match left front, reversing all
shapings and position of patterns and working buttonholes to correspond with buttons
as follows:
Buttonhole row 1 (RS) Moss/seed st 2, cast/
bind off 2, patt to end.
Buttonhole row 2 Patt to end, casting on 2
sts over those cast/bound off in previous
row.

SLEEVES
Using larger needles and A used double cast
on 71 sts.
Foundation row 1 (WS) P to end.
Row 1 For moss/seed st [k1, p1] twice, work
row 1 of pattern No 2 over next 12 sts, work
row 1 of pattern No 1 over next 10 sts, work
row 1 of pattern No 3 over next 19 sts, work
row 1 of pattern No 1 over next 10 sts, work
row 1 of pattern No 2 over next 12 sts, for
moss/seed st [p1, k1] twice.
Row 2 For moss/seed st [k1, p1] twice, work
row 2 of pattern No 2 over next 12 sts, work
row 2 of pattern No 1 over next 10 sts, work
row 2 of pattern No 3 over next 19 sts, work
row 2 of pattern No 1 over next 10 sts, work
row 2 of pattern No 2 over next 12 sts, for
moss/seed st [p1, k1] twice.
Cont straight in patt as set until sleeve
measures 6cm/2½in from cast-on edge, ending with a WS row.
To reverse the cuff, cut off yarn, slip sts from
one needle to the other, then beg with the
same row cont in patt for 6cm/2½in more.
Inc and work into moss/seed st, 1 st at each
end of the next and every foll 12th row until
there are 87 sts.
Work without shaping until sleeve measures

46cm/18in from beg at cast-on edge, ending with a WS row.

Shape top

Cast/bind off 5 sts at the beg of the next 2 rows.

Dec 1 st at each end of the next and every foll alt row until 35 sts rem.

Cast/bind off 3 sts at beg of next 2 rows and 4 sts at beg of foll 2 rows.

Cast/bind off 5 sts at beg of next 3 rows then cast/bind off rem 6 sts.

LEFT COLLAR

Using larger needles and A used double cast on 2 sts.

Row 1 K1, p1.

Row 2 P1, k1.

These 2 rows set the moss/seed st patt.

Inc and work into moss/seed st 1 st at each end of the next and 2 foll 4th rows. 5 sts.

These 5 sts form the front edge and will rem in moss/seed st for remainder of collar.

Inc and work in reversed st st, 1 st at each end of every foll 4th row until there are 20 sts.

Work straight until sloping edge of collar fits along sloping edge of left front.

Cast/bind off.

RIGHT COLLAR

Work to match left collar reversing all shapings.

EDGINGS

Using smaller needles and B used double cast on 7 sts. Work in st st until band is long enough to fit all around outside edge of jacket. Cast/bind off.

Make edgings for pocket tops and lower edges of sleeves.

FINISHING

Join left shoulder seams. With right sides of collars to wrong sides of fronts, sew collars in place with cast-on sts to cast/bound off sts at beg of neck shaping and so reversed st st folds on to right side of jacket. Sew in sleeves.

Sew the pocket in place. Join the side and the sleeve seams.

Sew row ends of edging to edge of garment on right side, then fold edging to wrong side and sew opposite row ends in place, enclosing edge of garment.

Fold the collars to the right side and sew rem 2 buttons to corners to secure collar to jacket.

CAMBRIDGE

I LOVE THE SIMPLE, LONG LINES OF THIS SWEATER. THE

TRIANGULAR SHAPES ARE ECHOED THROUGH THE CABLES AND

THE SILHOUETTE, WITH THE WIDE NECK AND SHOULDERS

GRACEFULLY TAPERING TO THE HEM.

◆

MATERIALS
600g/21¼oz of a double knitting (US worsted weight) wool
Pair each of 3¼mm (US 3) and 4mm (US 6) knitting needles
Cable needle

MEASUREMENTS
Actual measurements
Bust 100cm/40in
Length to shoulders 68cm/26¾in
Sleeve seam 56cm/22in

TENSION/GAUGE
24 sts and 32 rows to 10cm/4in measured over patt worked on 4mm (US 6) needles

Please check your tension/gauge carefully and change needle size if necessary

BACK
Using smaller needles cast on 120 sts.
Work in patt as follows:
Row 1 P2, k6, p2, * k1, p2, k6, p2, rep from * to end.
Row 2 K2, p6, k2, * p1, k2, p6, k2, rep from * to end.
Rows 3 to 6 Rep rows 1 and 2 twice more.
Row 7 P2, C6B (see page 159), p2, * k1, p2, C6B, p2, rep from * to end.
Row 8 As row 2.
These 8 rows set the patt.
Rep these 8 rows 4 times more.

Change to larger needles and work as follows:
Next row K11, patt to last 11 sts, k11.
Next row P11, patt to last 11 sts, p11.
Work 14 more rows as set.
Next row K22, patt to last 22 sts, k22.
Next row P22, patt to last 22 sts, p22.
Work 14 more rows as set.
Next row K33, patt to last 33 sts, k33.
Next row P33, patt to last 33 sts, p33.
Work 14 more rows as set.
Next row K44, patt to last 44 sts, k44.
Next row P44, patt to last 44 sts, p44.
Work 14 more rows as set.
Next row K55, patt to last 55 sts, k55.
Next row P55, patt to last 55 sts, p55.
Work 14 more rows as set.
Next row K to end.
Next row P to end.
Beg with a k row continue working in stocking/stockinette stitch until back measures 44.5cm/17½in from cast-on edge, ending with a p row.
Shape armholes
Dec 1 st at each end of the next and every foll alt row until 102 sts rem.
Continue working in stocking/stockinette stitch without shaping until the back measures 68cm/26¾in from the beg at cast-on edge, ending with a WS row.
Shape shoulders
Cast/bind off 12 sts at beg of next 4 rows.
Cast/bind off rem 54 sts.

FRONT

Work as given for back until front measures 64cm/25¼in from beg ending with a WS row.

Shape neck

Next row Patt 40 sts, turn and leave rem sts on a spare needle.

** Cast/bind off 4 sts at beg of next and 3 foll alt rows. 24 sts.

Cont straight until front measures the same as back to shoulder ending at armhole edge.

Shape shoulder

Cast/bind off 12 sts at beg of next row.

Work 1 row.

Cast/bind off rem 12 sts. **

With right side facing join yarn to rem sts and cast/bind off next 22 sts, patt to end.

Work 1 row.

Complete to match first side from ** to **.

SLEEVES

Using smaller needles cast on 60 sts.

Work in patt as follows:

Row 1 P2, * k1, p2, k6, p2, rep from * to last 3 sts, k1, p2.

Row 2 K2, * p1, k2, p6, k2, rep from * to last 3 sts, p1, k2.

Rows 3 to 6 Rep rows 1 and 2 twice more.

Row 7 P2, * k1, p2, C6B, p2, rep from * to last 3 sts, k1, p2.

Row 8 As row 2.

These 8 rows set the patt.

Rep these 8 rows 4 times more.

Change to larger needles and work 8 rows more in patt as set.

Next row K14, patt to last 14 sts, k14.

Next row P14, patt to last 14 sts, p14.

Work 14 more rows as set **at the same time**

inc 1 st at each end of the next and 3 foll 4th rows. 68 sts.

Next row K29, patt to last 29 sts, k29.

Next row P29, patt to last 29 sts, p29.

Cont in patt as set, increasing 1 st at each end of the next and every foll 4th row until there are 120 sts.

Cont straight until sleeve measures 56cm/22in from cast-on edge, ending with a WS row.

Shape top

Cast/bind off 55 sts at beg of next 2 rows.

Work 7.5cm/3in more in cable patt on rem 10 sts.

Cast/bind off.

NECKBAND

Using larger needles cast on 20 sts.

Row 1 P2, k6, p2, k1, p9.

Row 2 K9, p1, k2, p6, k2.

Rows 3 to 6 Rep rows 1 and 2 twice more.

Row 7 P2, C6B, p2, k1, p9.

Row 8 As row 2.

Rep these 8 rows until neckband fits around neck edge, ending with row 8.

Cast/bind off.

FINISHING

Sew in sleeves, sewing last 7.5cm/3in at top of sleeve to sts cast/bound off shoulder.

Join cast on and cast/bound off edge of neckband together.

With right sides together, sew 'p2' edge of neckband to edge.

Fold neckband in half and sew other edge of neckband to seamline.

Join side and sleeve seams.

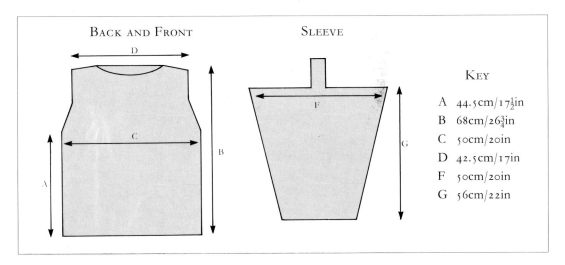

BACK AND FRONT	SLEEVE	KEY

KEY

A 44.5cm/17½in

B 68cm/26¾in

C 50cm/20in

D 42.5cm/17in

F 50cm/20in

G 56cm/22in

CLUB

———————◆———————

WOOD-PANELLED DRAWING ROOMS AND
THE LIBRARIES OF CLUBS SET OFF NICELY
THE SOFT TEXTURES OF MY COTTON AND
WOOL KNITWEAR. IN THE EIGHT SWEATERS
AND CARDIGANS THAT FOLLOW YOU WILL
SEE THE INFLUENCE OF TRADITIONAL
CHECKS AND TWEED, AMERICAN INDIAN
DESIGNS, SCOTTISH FAIR ISLE PATTERNS,
KELIMS, AND EVEN THE EMBROIDERIES
OF THE KUBA TRIBE OF ZAIRE.

NEWMARKET

THIS IS AN INTRICATE ARAN DESIGN FOR WARMTH AND

DURABILITY. WITH ITS VERSATILE SHAWL COLLAR AND SUEDE

ELBOW PATCHES THIS IS A SWEATER FOR LOVERS OF THE

GREAT OUTDOORS.

———————◆———————

MATERIALS

600g/21¼oz of a 2 ply (US fingering) Shetland wool
Pair each of 2¼mm (US 1) and 3mm (US 3) knitting needles
Cable needle
2 buttons
2 suede elbow patches

MEASUREMENTS

Actual measurements
Chest 112cm/44in
Length to shoulders 66cm/26in
Sleeve seam 52cm/20½in

TENSION/GAUGE

36 sts and 42 rows to 10cm/4in measured over patt worked on 3mm (US 3) needles

Please check your tension/gauge carefully and change needle size if necessary

Pattern No 1 (worked over 8 sts)
Row 1 P1, k1 tbl, p1, k1, yo, k1, p1, k1 tbl, p1.
Row 2 K1, p1 tbl, k1, p3, k1, p1 tbl, k1.
Row 3 P1, k1 tbl, p1, k3, pass first of these sts over 2nd and 3rd st and off the needle, p1, k1 tbl, p1.
Row 4 K1, p1 tbl, k1, p2, k1, p1 tbl, k1.
These 4 rows form the patt.
Note: When counting sts, always count this panel as 8 sts.

Pattern No 2 (worked over 6 sts)
Row 1 K2, [sl 1 purlwise] twice, k2.
Row 2 P2, [sl 1 purlwise] twice, p2.
Row 3 and 4 As rows 1 and 2.
Row 5 Slip next 2 sts on to cable needle and leave at back of work, k1, k2 from cable needle, slip next st on to cable needle and leave at front of work, k2, k1 from cable needle.
Row 6 P6.
These 6 rows form the patt.

Pattern No 3 (worked over 6 sts)
Row 1 K6.
Row 2 P6.
Row 3 C6F (see page 159).
Row 4 P6.
Rows 5 to 8 Rep rows 1 and 2 twice more.
These 8 rows form the patt.

BACK

Using smaller needles cast on 138 sts.
Rib row 1 (RS) K2, * p2, k2, rep from * to end.
Rib row 2 P2, * k2, p2, rep from * to end.
Rep these 2 rows for 8.5cm/3¼in ending with rib row 1.
Inc row Rib 6, * M1, rib 2, rep from * to last 6 sts, M1, rib 6. 202 sts.
Change to larger needles.
Work in patt as follows:
Row 1 For moss/seed st [p1, k1] 3 times, work row 1 of pattern No 1 over next 8 sts, *

work row 1 of pattern No 2 over next 6 sts, work row 1 of pattern No 1 over next 8 sts, work row 1 of pattern No 3 over next 6 sts, work row 1 of pattern No 1 over next 8 sts, rep from * 5 times more, work row 1 of pattern No 2 over next 6 sts, work row 1 of pattern No 1 over next 8 sts, then for moss/seed st [k1, p1] 3 times.

Row 2 For moss/seed st [p1, k1] 3 times, work row 2 of pattern No 1 over next 8 sts, * work row 2 of pattern No 2 over next 6 sts, work row 2 of pattern No 1 over next 8 sts, work row 2 of pattern No 3 over next 6 sts, work row 2 of of pattern No 1 over next 8 sts, rep from * 5 times more, work row 2 of pattern No 2 over next 6 sts, work row 2 of pattern No 1 over next 8 sts, then for moss/seed st [k1, p1] 3 times.

Cont straight in patt as set until back measures 40.5cm/16in from cast-on edge, ending with a WS row.

Shape armholes
Cast/bind off 7 sts at beg of next 2 rows.
Dec 1 st each end of the next and every foll alt row until 162 sts rem. **
Cont straight in patt until back measures 66cm/26in from cast-on edge, ending with a WS row.

Shape shoulders
Cast/bind off 15 sts at beg of next 6 rows.
Cast/bind off rem 72 sts.

FRONT
Work as given for back to **.
Patt 1 row, ending with a WS row.

Shape neck
Next row Patt 89 sts, turn and leave rem sts on a spare needle.
Cast on 16 sts.
Next row P16, patt to end.
Next row Patt to last 16 sts, k16.
***Inc and work into the st st band at centre 1 st on next and every foll 3rd row until there are 129 sts.
Cont straight until front measures same as back to shoulder ending at armhole edge.
Shape shoulder
Cast/bind off 15 sts at beg of next and 2 foll alt rows. 84 sts.
Work straight in patt as set for 10cm/4in more, ending with a WS row.
Leave these sts on a spare needle. ***

Cast on 32 sts, k the 32 sts just cast on, then with right side facing patt to end of rem sts of front.
Next row Patt to last 16 sts, p16.
Next row K16, patt to end.
Complete to match first side from *** to ***.
Graft the two sets of stitches together.

SLEEVES
Using smaller needles cast on 78 sts.
Work 10cm/4in rib as given for back, ending with a RS row.
Inc row Rib 2, * M1, rib 5, rep from * to last st, M1, rib 1. 94 sts.

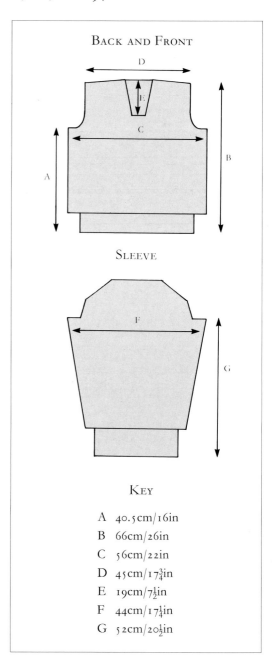

BACK AND FRONT

SLEEVE

KEY

A 40.5cm/16in
B 66cm/26in
C 56cm/22in
D 45cm/17¾in
E 19cm/7½in
F 44cm/17¼in
G 52cm/20½in

Change to larger needles.

Work in patt as follows:

Row 1 Work last 2 sts of row 1 of pattern No 1 over next 2 sts, * work row 1 of pattern No 3 over next 6 sts, work row 1 of pattern No 1 over next 8 sts, work row 1 of pattern No 2 over next 6 sts, work row 1 of pattern No 1 over next 8 sts, rep from * twice more, work row 1 of pattern No 3 over next 6 sts, work first 2 sts of row 1 of pattern No 1 over next 2 sts.

Row 2 Work last 2 sts of row 2 of pattern No 1 over next 2 sts, * work row 2 of pattern No 3 over next 6 sts, work row 2 of pattern No 1 over next 8 sts, work row 2 of pattern No 2 over next 6 sts, work row 2 of pattern No 1 over next 8 sts, rep from * twice more, work row 2 of pattern No 3 over next 6 sts, work first 2 sts of row 2 of pattern No 1 over next 2 sts.

These 2 rows set the patt.

Inc and work into patt 1 st each end of the next and every foll 5th row until there are 158 sts.

Work straight until sleeve measures 52cm/ 20½in from cast-on edge, ending with a WS row.

Shape top

Cast/bind off 7 sts at beg of next 2 rows. Dec 1 st at each end of the next 50 rows. 44 sts. Cast/bind off.

FINISHING

Join shoulder seams. Sew in sleeves. Sew suede patches to back half of sleeves at elbow level. Join side and sleeve seams. Fold st st section of collar to wrong side and stitch loosely in place. Lap left side of collar over right and stitch neatly in place. Sew on buttons and make button loops to match.

ROEHAMPTON

WHEN DESIGNING THIS SWEATER I WAS THINKING OF OLD

COUNTRY HOUSES AND THE BRIGHT CHECKS AND EARTHY TWEEDS

THAT WERE WORN IN THEIR DRAUGHTY CORRIDORS.

◆

MATERIALS
400g/14oz of a double knitting (US worsted weight) wool in main colour A
300g/10½oz in contrast colour B
50g/1¾oz each in contrast colours C and D
Pair each of 3¼mm (US 3) and 4½mm (US 7) knitting needles
3 buttons

MEASUREMENTS
Actual measurements
Bust 106cm/41½in
Length to shoulders 61cm/24in
Sleeve seam (adjustable) 53cm/21in

TENSION/GAUGE
24 sts and 24 rows to 10cm/4in measured over patt worked on 4½mm (US 7) needles

Please check your tension/gauge carefully and change needle size if necessary

NOTE
When working from chart use separate small balls of yarn for each isolated vertical line in C and twist yarns together at WS of work when changing colour to avoid making a hole.

BACK
Using smaller needles and A cast on 87 sts.
Rib row 1 (RS) K1, * p1, k1, rep from * to end.
Rib row 2 P1, * k1, p1, rep from * to end.

Rep these 2 rows for 6cm/2½in ending with rib row 1.
Inc row Rib 4, * M1, rib 2, rep from * to last 5 sts, M1, rib 5. 127 sts.
Change to larger needles.
Work in patt from chart as follows:
Row 1 Work last 2 sts of row 1, then work 27 st patt rep 4 times, then work first 17 sts of row 1.
Row 2 Work last 17 sts of row 2, work 27 st patt rep 4 times, work first 2 sts of row 2.
Cont straight in patt as set until back measures 30.5cm/12in from cast-on edge, ending with a WS row.
Shape armholes
Dec 1 st at each end of the next and every foll alt row until 105 sts rem.
Cont straight in patt until back measures 61cm/24in from cast-on edge, ending with a WS row.
Shape neck and shoulders
Next row Patt 34 sts, turn and leave rem sts on a spare needle.
Next row Work 2 tog, patt to end.
Next row Cast/bind off 16 sts, patt to last 2 sts, work 2 tog.
Cast/bind off rem 16 sts.
With right side facing return to sts on spare needle, cast/bind off 37 sts, patt to end.
Next row Cast/bind off 16 sts, patt to last 2 sts, work 2 tog.
Next row Work 2 tog, patt to end.
Cast/bind off rem 16 sts.

POCKET LININGS (make 2)

Using larger needles and A cast on 31 sts.
Work 12cm/4¾in in st st ending with a p row.
Leave sts on a spare needle.

LEFT FRONT

Using smaller needles and A cast on 43 sts.
Work 6cm/2½in rib as given for back ending
with a RS row.
Inc row Rib 3, * M1, rib 2, rep from * to end.
63 sts.
Change to larger needles.
Work in patt from chart as follows:
Row 1 Work 27 st patt rep of row 1 twice,
then work first 9 sts of row 1.
Row 2 Work last 9 sts of row 2, then work 27
st patt rep twice.
Cont in patt as set until front measures 9cm/
3½in from cast-on edge ending with a WS
row.
**Shape neck
Dec 1 st at neck edge of next row and 19 foll
6th rows *at the same time* when front 18cm/
7¼in from cast-on edge, ending at armhole
edge, place pocket as follows:
Next row Patt 16 sts, slip next 31 sts on to a
holder, then patt across 31 sts from one
pocket lining, patt to end.
Cont to dec at neck edge as before, work in
patt until front measures the same as back to
armhole shaping ending at armhole edge,
then shape armhole by decreasing 1 st at this
edge on every alt row 11 times in all. Cont to
dec at neck edge as before until 32 sts rem,
then work straight in patt until front measures the same as back to shoulder shaping
ending at armhole edge.
Shape shoulder
Cast/bind off 16 sts at beg of next row.
Work 1 row.
Cast/bind off rem 16 sts. **

RIGHT FRONT

Using smaller needles and A cast on 43 sts.
Work 6cm/2½in rib as given for back ending
with a RS row.
Inc row Rib 3, * M1, rib 2, rep from * to end.
63 sts.
Change to larger needles.
Work in patt from chart as follows:
Note: For right front only read odd-
numbered rows from left to right and even-
numbered rows from right to left to reverse
patt.
Row 1 Work last 9 sts of row 1, then work 27
st patt rep twice.
Row 2 Work 27 st patt rep twice, then work
first 9 sts of row 2.
Cont in patt as set until front measures 9cm/
3½in from cast-on edge ending with a WS
row.
Complete as given for left front from **
to **.

SLEEVES

Using smaller needles and A cast on 45 sts.
Work 6cm/2½in rib as given for back, ending
with a RS row.
Inc row Rib 5, * M1, rib 5, rep from * to end.
53 sts.

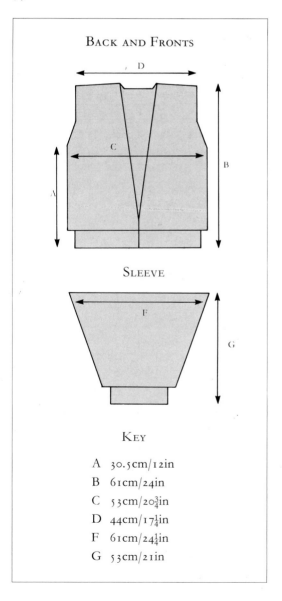

BACK AND FRONTS

SLEEVE

KEY

A 30.5cm/12in

B 61cm/24in

C 53cm/20¾in

D 44cm/17¼in

F 61cm/24¼in

G 53cm/21in

Change to larger needles.

Work to patt from chart as follows:

Row 1 Work last 6 sts of row 1, then work 27 st patt rep once, then work first 20 sts of row 1.

Row 2 Work last 20 sts of row 2, then work 27 st patt once, then work first 6 sts of row 2.

Keeping patt correct, inc and work into patt 1 st each end of the next and every foll alt row until there are 147 sts.

Work straight until sleeve measures 53cm/ 21in from cast-on edge, ending with a WS row.

Cast/bind off.

FRONT BAND

Join shoulders.

Using smaller needles and A cast on 11 sts.

Rib row 1 K2, [p1, k1] 4 times, k1.

Rib row 2 K1, [p1, k1] 5 times.

Cont in rib until band when slightly stretched fits up left front across back neck and down sloping edge of right front to beg of neck shaping.

Sew band in place.

Sew on buttons to left front, the first to come 1.5cm/½in from the lower edge, the third level with the first row of the neck shaping and the remaining one spaced evenly between the first and third.

Work buttonholes to correspond with buttons as follows:

Buttonhole row 1 Rib 4, cast/bind off 3 sts, rib to end.

Buttonhole row 2 Rib 4, cast on 3 sts, rib to end.

Cont in rib, until band reaches cast-on edge of right front.

Cast/bind off.

POCKET TOPS

With right side facing using smaller needles and A, k across sts from holder. 31 sts.

Work 5 rows rib as given for back.

Cast/bind off in rib.

FINISHING

Set in sleeves. Join side and sleeve seams.

Sew pockets and row ends of pocket tops in place.

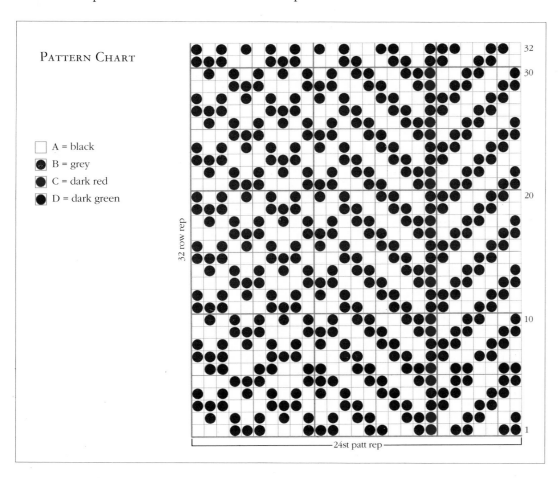

PATTERN CHART

☐ A = black
● B = grey
● C = dark red
● D = dark green

32 row rep

24st patt rep

GARRICK

THE SOURCES I USED FOR THIS TRULY

DRAMATIC SMOKING JACKET WERE

THE INCREDIBLE EMBROIDERIES OF

THE KUBA TRIBE OF ZAIRE.

◆

MATERIALS
650g/23oz of a double knitting (US worsted weight) wool in each of colours A and B
100g/3½oz each of contrast colours C, D and E
50g/1¾oz each of contrast colours F, G and H
Pair each of 3¼mm (US 3) and 4mm (US 6) knitting needles
1 large button
1 small button

MEASUREMENTS
Actual measurements
Bust 110cm/43½in
Length to shoulders 79cm/31in
Sleeve seam 48cm/19in

TENSION/GAUGE
28 sts and 28 rows to 10cm/4in measured over patt worked on 4mm (US 6) needles

Please check your tension/gauge carefully and change needle size if necessary

NOTE
When working from chart use separate small balls of yarn for each isolated area of colour and twist yarns together at WS of work when changing colour to avoid making a hole.

BACK
Using smaller needles and A, cast on 110 sts.
Starting with a k row, work 4cm/1½in st st,

ending with a k row.

P 3 rows.

Change to larger needles.

Work in st st in patt from chart as foll:

Row 1 (RS) Work last 7 sts of row 1, then work 48 st patt rep twice, then work first 7 sts of row 1.

Row 2 Work last 7 sts of row 2, then work 48 st patt rep twice, then work first 7 sts of row 2.

These 2 rows set the patt.

Keeping patt correct, inc and work into patt 1 st each end of the 11th and every foll 6th row until there are 154 sts.

Work straight in patt until back measures 54cm/21¼in from cast-on edge, ending with a WS row.

Shape armholes

Row 1 K2, sl 1, k1, psso, patt to last 4 sts, k2 tog, k2.

Row 2 Patt to end.

Rep the last 2 rows 6 times more. 140 sts.

Cont straight in patt until back measures 83.5cm/33in from cast-on edge, ending with a WS row.

Shape shoulders

Cast/bind off 45 sts at beg of next 2 rows.

Cast/bind off rem 50 sts.

POCKET LININGS (make 2)

Using larger needles and A cast on 38 sts.

Work 14.5cm/5¾in in st st, ending with a p row.

Leave these sts on a holder

LEFT FRONT

Using smaller needles and A, cast on 66 sts.

Starting with a K row, work 4cm/1½in st st, ending with a k row. P 2 rows.

Next row Cast on 22 sts, p these sts, then p across 66 sts on needle.

Change to larger needles.

Work in st st in patt from chart as foll:

Row 1 (RS) Work last 7 sts of row 1, then work 48 st patt rep once, then work first 33 sts of row 1.

Row 2 Work last 33 sts of row 2, then work 48 st patt rep once, then work first 7 sts of row 2.

These 2 rows set the patt.

Keeping patt correct, inc and work into patt 1 st at side edge of the 11th and every foll 6th row 22 times in all *at the same time* when front measures 23cm/9in from cast-on edge, ending with a p row, place pocket as follows:

Next row Patt 4 sts, slip next 38 sts on to a holder, patt across 38 sts of one pocket lining, then patt to end.

Keeping patt correct cont to inc as before until front measures 40cm/15¾in from cast-on edge, ending with a k row.

Cast on 35 sts for collar facing, patt across

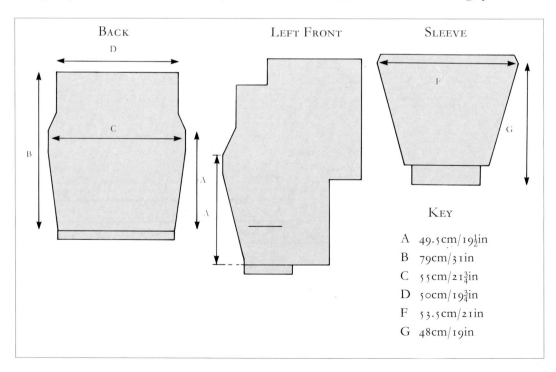

| BACK | LEFT FRONT | SLEEVE |

KEY

A 49.5cm/19½in

B 79cm/31in

C 55cm/21¾in

D 50cm/19¾in

F 53.5cm/21in

G 48cm/19in

these sts, then patt to end.

Cont in patt until incs at side edge have been completed. 145 sts.

Work straight in patt until front measures 54cm/21¼in from cast-on edge, ending with a WS row.

Shape armhole

Row 1 K2, sl 1, k1, psso, patt to end.

Row 2 Patt to end.

Rep the last 2 rows 6 times more. 138 sts.

Cont straight in patt until front measures 83.5cm/33in from cast-on edge, ending with a WS row.

Shape shoulder

Cast/bind off 45 sts at beg of next row, patt to end. 93 sts.

Cont in patt on these sts for 10cm/4in more. Cast/bind off.

RIGHT FRONT

Using smaller needles and A, cast on 66 sts.

Starting with a K row, work 4cm/1½in st st, ending with a k row.

P 1 row.

Next row Cast on 22 sts, p these sts, then p across 66 sts on needle.

P 1 row.

Change to larger needles.

Work in st st in patt from chart as foll:

Row 1 (RS) Work last 33 sts of row 1, then work 48 st patt rep once, then work first 7 sts of row 1.

Row 2 Work last 7 sts of row 2, then work 48 st patt rep once, then work first 33 sts of row 2.

These 2 rows set the patt.

Keeping patt correct, inc and work into patt 1 st at side edge of the 11th and every foll 6th row 22 times in all *at the same time* when front measures 23cm/9in from cast-on edge, ending with a p row, place pocket as follows:

Next row Patt to last 42 sts, slip next 38 sts on to a holder, patt across 38 sts of one pocket lining, then patt to end.

Keeping patt correct cont to inc as before until front measures 32.5cm/12¾in from cast-on edge, ending with a p row.

Make buttonhole as follows:

Next row Patt 22 sts, turn and leave rem sts on a spare needle. Work a further 8 rows on these sts. Break off yarn.

Return to sts on spare needle, join on yarn

and cont to inc as set, work 10 rows in patt, then patt across 22 sts.

Complete as for left front reversing all shapings.

SLEEVES

Using smaller needles and A, cast on 58 sts.

Rib row 1 K2, * p2, k2, rep from * to end.

Rib row 2 P2, * k2, p2, rep from * to end.

Rep these 2 rows for 8cm/3in, ending with rib row 1.

Inc row Rib 3, * M1, rib 2, M1, rib 3, rep from * to end. 80 sts.

Change to larger needles.

Work in st st in patt from chart as foll:

Row 1 (RS) Work last 16 sts of row 11, then work 48 st patt rep once, then work first 16 sts of row 11.

Row 2 Work last 16 sts of row 12, then work 48 st patt rep once, then work first 16 sts of row 12.

These 2 rows set the patt.

Keeping patt correct, inc and work into patt 1 st at each end of the next and every foll 3rd row until there are 150 sts.

Cont straight in patt until sleeve measures 48cm/19in from cast-on edge, ending with a WS row.

Shape top

Row 1 K2, sl 1, k1, psso, patt to end.

Row 2 Patt to end.

Rep the last 2 rows 6 times more.

Cast/bind off.

POCKET TOPS

With right side facing using smaller needles and A, k across 38 sts from holder. Work 5 rows rib as given for sleeves.

Cast/bind off in rib.

FINISHING

Join shoulder seams. Sew in sleeves. Join side and sleeve seams. Fold up hem around lower edge and sew in place. Join cast/bound off edges of collar extension. Sew row ends to back neck. Fold collar and facing in half and sew neatly in place.

Sew large button to left front level with buttonhole and 12cm/4¾in from foldline. Buttonhole stitch around buttonhole, then make a button loop on left front level with button.

Sew small button to back of right front to match button loop.

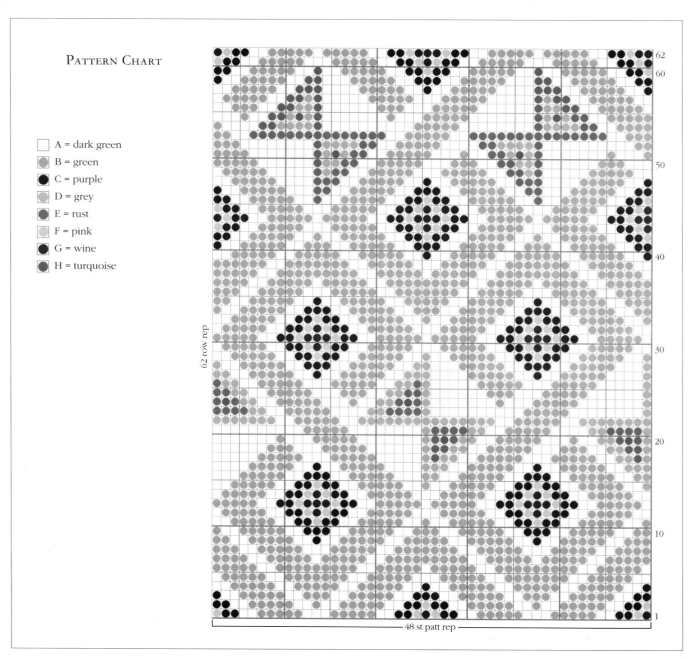

PATTERN CHART

A = dark green
B = green
C = purple
D = grey
E = rust
F = pink
G = wine
H = turquoise

62 row rep

48 st patt rep

CHELSEA

THIS SWEATER BRINGS TO MIND THE COLOURS OF AN

EARLY AUTUMN EVENING — THE BRIGHT, JEWEL COLOURS OF THE

CHANGING LEAVES, ALMOST LUMINOUS AGAINST THE

DARKENING GLOW OF THE EVENING SKY.

———————◆———————

MATERIALS
600g/21¼oz of a lightweight double knitting (US sport weight) wool in main colour A
50g/1¾oz each in contrast colours B, C, D, E, F and G
Pair each of 3mm (US 2) and 3¾mm (US 5) knitting needles
5 buttons

MEASUREMENTS
Actual measurements
Bust 100cm/39½in
Length to shoulders 68.5cm/27in
Sleeve seam (adjustable) 56cm/22in

TENSION/GAUGE
28 sts and 32 rows to 10cm/4in measured over patt worked on 3¾mm (US 5) needles

Please check your tension/gauge carefully and change needle size if necessary

NOTE
When working from charts use separate small balls of yarn for each isolated area of colour and twist yarns together at WS of work when changing colour to avoid making a hole.

BACK
Using smaller needles and A cast on 122 sts.
Rib row 1 (RS) K2, * p2, k2, rep from * to end.
Rib row 2 P2, * k2, p2, rep from * to end.

Rep these 2 rows for 6cm/2½in ending with rib row 1.
Inc row Rib 7, * M1, rib 6, rep from * to last 7 sts, M1, rib 7. 141 sts.
Change to larger needles. K1 row B and p1 row C.
Cont in st st in patt from chart No 1 as foll:
Row 3 (RS) Work last 6 sts of row 3, then work 26 st patt rep 5 times, then work first 5 sts of row 3.
Row 4 Work last 5 sts of row 4, then work 26 st patt rep 5 times, then work first 6 sts of row 4.
Cont in patt as set until row 34 has been worked. Then work 10 rows in st st with A only. Now work from chart No 2, repeating rows 1 to 72 to form the patt.
Cont straight in patt until back measures 43cm/17in from cast-on edge, ending with a WS row.
Shape armholes
Cast/bind off 4 sts at beg of next 2 rows.
Keeping continuity of patt dec 1 st at each end of the next 4 rows. 125 sts.
Cont straight in patt until back measures 68.5cm/27in from cast-on edge, ending with a WS row.
Shape shoulders
Cast/bind off 39 sts at beg of next 2 rows.
Cast/bind off rem 47 sts.

POCKET LININGS (make 2)
Using larger needles and A cast on 35 sts.

Work 13cm/5in in st st, ending with a p row.
Leave sts on a spare needle.

LEFT FRONT

Using smaller needles and A cast on 58 sts.
Work 6cm/2½in rib as given for back ending with a RS row.

Inc row Rib 4, * M1, rib 5, M1, rib 4, rep from * to end. 70 sts.
Change to larger needles. K1 row B and p1 row C.
Cont in st st in patt from chart No 1 as foll:
Row 3 (RS) Work last 6 sts of row 3, then work 26 st patt rep twice, then work first 12 sts of row 3.
Row 4 Work last 12 sts of row 4, then work 26 st patt rep twice, then work first 6 sts of row 4.
Cont in patt as set until row 34 has been worked.
Using A work 4 rows st st.

Place pocket
Next row (RS) K 18 sts, slip next 35 sts on to a holder, then k across 35 sts from one pocket lining, patt rem 17 sts.
Using A work 5 rows st st.
Now work from chart No 2 as follows:
Row 1 (RS) With A, k20, p2, k8, p2, k38.
Omitting the motifs at centre of chart work in patt as set until front measures 34cm/13½in from cast-on edge ending with a RS row.

**Shape neck
Dec 1 st at neck edge of next row and 22 foll 3rd rows *at the same time* when front measures the same as back to armhole shaping ending at armhole edge shape armhole by casting/binding off 4 sts at beg of next row, then dec 1 st at armhole edge on the next 4 rows.
Cont straight in patt until front measures the same as back to shoulder shaping ending at armhole edge.

Shape shoulder
Cast/bind off rem 39 sts. **

RIGHT FRONT

Using smaller needles and A cast on 58 sts.
Work 6cm/2½in rib as given for back ending with a RS row.
Inc row Rib 4, * M1, rib 5, M1, rib 4, rep from * to end. 70 sts.

Change to larger needles. K1 row B and p1 row C.
Cont in st st in patt from chart No 1 as foll:
Row 3 (RS) Work last 13 sts of row 3, then work 26 st patt rep twice, then work first 5 sts of row 3.
Row 4 Work first 5 sts of row 4, then work 26 st patt rep twice, then work first 13 sts of row 4.
Cont in patt as set until row 34 has been worked.
Using A work 4 rows st st.
Place pocket
Next row (RS) K 17 sts, slip next 35 sts on to a holder, then k across 35 sts from one pocket lining, patt rem 18 sts.
Using A work 5 rows st st.

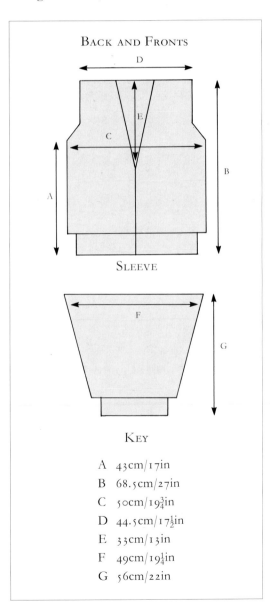

BACK AND FRONTS

SLEEVE

KEY

A 43cm/17in
B 68.5cm/27in
C 50cm/19¾in
D 44.5cm/17½in
E 33cm/13in
F 49cm/19¼in
G 56cm/22in

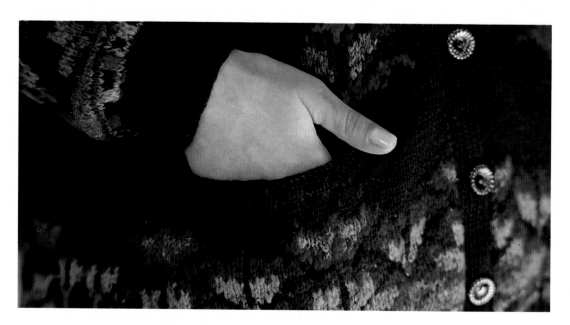

Now work from chart No 2 as follows:
Row 1 (RS) With A, k38, p2, k8, p2, k20.
Omitting the motifs at centre of chart work in patt as set until front measures 34cm/13½in from cast-on edge ending with a RS row.
Complete as given for left front from ** to **.

SLEEVES

Using smaller needles and A cast on 46 sts.
Work 6cm/2½in rib as given for back, ending with a RS row.
Inc row Rib 2, * M1, rib 2, M1, rib 3, rep from * to last 4 sts, [M1, rib 2] twice. 64 sts.
Change to smaller needles. K1 row B and p1 row C.
Cont in st st in patt from chart No 1 as foll:
Row 3 (RS) Work last 19 sts of row 3, then work 26 st patt rep once, then work first 19 sts of row 3.
Row 4 Work last 19 sts of row 4, then work 26 st patt once, then work first 19 sts of row 4.
Keeping patt correct, inc and work into patt 1 st each end of the next row and 10 foll 4th rows, working in A only after 34th chart row has been completed.
There are 86 sts on the needle.
Now work in patt from chart No 2 as follows:
Starting on row 38, work the 86 sts as marked on the centre of chart.
Keeping continuity of patt, cont inc and work into patt, 1 st at each end of every foll 4th row until there are 138 sts.
Work straight until sleeve measures 56cm/22in from cast-on edge, ending with a WS row.
Cast/bind off.

FRONT BAND
Join shoulders
Using smaller needles and A cast on 11 sts.
Rib row 1 K2, [p1, k1] 4 times, k1.
Rib row 2 K1, [p1, k1] 5 times.
Rep the last 2 rows once more.
***Buttonhole row 1** Rib 4, cast/bind off 3 sts, rib to end.
Buttonhole row 2 Rib 4, cast on 3 sts, rib to end.
Work in rib for 8cm/3in. ***
Work from *** to *** 3 times more.
Rep the 2 buttonhole rows once more.
Cont in rib until band when slightly stretched fits up right front across back neck and down left front.

POCKET TOPS
With right side facing using smaller needles and A, decreasing 1 st at centre, k across sts from holder. 34 sts.
Work 5 rows rib as given for back.
Cast/bind off in rib.

FINISHING
Set in sleeves. Join side and sleeve seams.
Sew pockets and row ends of pocket ribs in place. Sew on front band. Sew on buttons.

Chart No 1

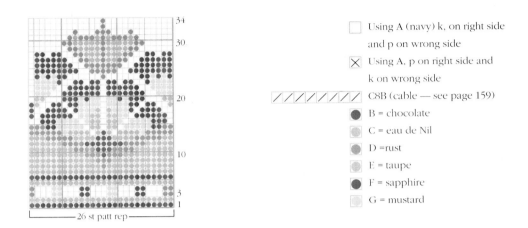

34
30
20
10
3
1

— 26 st patt rep —

Using A (navy) k, on right side and p on wrong side

Using A, p on right side and k on wrong side

C8B (cable — see page 159)

● B = chocolate
● C = eau de Nil
● D =rust
● E = taupe
● F = sapphire
● G = mustard

Chart No 2

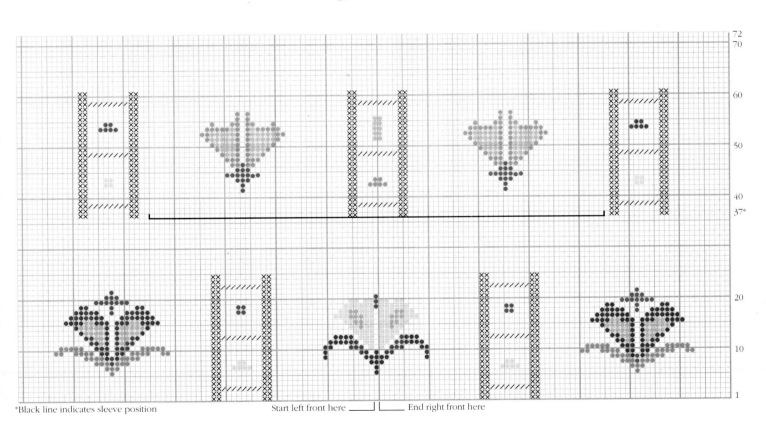

72
70
60
50
40
37*
20
10
1

*Black line indicates sleeve position

Start left front here ____| |____ End right front here

ALGONQUIN

THE DOLMAN SLEEVES CREATE A WIDE CANVAS ON WHICH TO

PAINT THIS CELEBRATION OF RICH COLOUR AND TEXTURE WHICH

IS A MARRIAGE OF AMERICAN INDIAN DESIGNS AND

TRADITIONAL SCOTTISH FAIR ISLES.

MATERIALS
400g/14oz of a 4 ply (US sport weight) wool in main colour A
50g/1¾oz each of contrast colours B, C, D, E, F, G, H, I, J, K and L
Pair each of 2¼mm (US 1) and 3¼mm (US 3) knitting needles

MEASUREMENTS
Actual measurements
Bust 100cm/39½in
Length to shoulders 57cm/22½in
Sleeve seam 56cm/22in

TENSION/GAUGE
30 sts and 32 rows to 10cm/4in measured over patt worked on 3¼mm (US 3) needles

Please check your tension/gauge carefully and change needle size if necessary

BACK
Using smaller needles and A, cast on 98 sts.
Rib row 1 (RS) K2, * p2, k2, rep from * to end.
Rib row 2 P2, * k2, p2, rep from * to end.
Rep these 2 rows for 6cm/2½in ending with rib row 1.
Inc row Rib 6, M1, * [rib 2, M1] twice, rib 1, M1, rep from * to last 7 sts, rib 2, M1, rib 5. 150 sts.
Change to larger needles.
Work in st st in patt from chart as foll:

Row 1 (RS) Work last 3 sts of row 1, then work 24 st patt rep 6 times, then work first 3 sts of row 1.
Row 2 Work last 3 sts of row 2, then work 24 st patt rep 6 times, then work first 3 sts of row 2.
Cont straight in patt until back measures 57cm/22½in from cast-on edge, ending with WS row.
Shape shoulders
Cast/bind off 24 sts at beg of next 2 rows and 25 sts at beg of foll 2 rows.
Leave rem 52 sts on a spare needle.

FRONT
Work as given for back until front measures 52cm/20½in from beg ending with a WS row.
Shape neck
Next row Patt 65 sts, turn and leave rem sts on a spare needle.
Dec 1 st at neck edge of next 16 rows.
Work 3 rows straight.
Shape shoulder
Cast/bind off 24 sts at beg of next row.
Work 1 row.
Cast/bind off rem 25 sts.
With right side facing return to rem sts and slip next 20 sts on to a spare needle, join on yarn, patt to end.
Dec 1 st at neck edge of next edge of next 16 rows.
Work 4 rows straight.
Shape shoulder

24 st patt rep 6 times, then work first 3 sts of row 68.

Keeping continuity of patt, inc and work into patt 1 st at each end of the next and every foll alt row until there are 200 sts. Work straight until sleeve measures 56cm/22in from cast-on edge, ending with a WS row. Cast/bind off.

NECKBAND
Join right shoulder seam.

With right side facing using smaller needles and A, pick up and k 29 sts down left side of front neck, 20 sts from front neck holder, pick up and k 29 sts up right side of front neck and 52 sts from back neck holder. 130 sts.

Work 6 rows in rib as given for back.
Cast/bind off in rib.

SHOULDER PADS (make 2)
Using 3¼mm needles and A, cast on 46 sts.
Work 15cm/6in in st st.
Cast/bind off.

FINISHING
Join left shoulder seam and neckband. Mark a point 33cm/13in down from shoulder seams on back and front, sew on sleeves between markers. Join side and sleeve seams. Fold shoulder pads in half diagonally and stitch along the two open sides. On the inside of the sweater, with the centre of the long edge to shoulder seam, sew the long edge to the sleeve seam. Sew the point to the shoulder seam.

Cast/bind off 24 sts at beg of next row.
Work 1 row. Cast/bind off rem 25 sts.

SLEEVES
Using smaller needles and A, cast on 50 sts.
Work 6cm/2½in rib as given for back, ending with a RS row.
Inc row Rib 3, * M1, rib 5, rep from * to last 2 sts, M1, rib 2. 60 sts.
Change to larger needles.
Work in st st in patt from chart as foll:
Row 1 (RS) Work lasts 6 sts of row 67, then work 24 st patt rep twice, then work first 6 sts of row 67.
Row 2 Work last 3 sts of row 68, then work

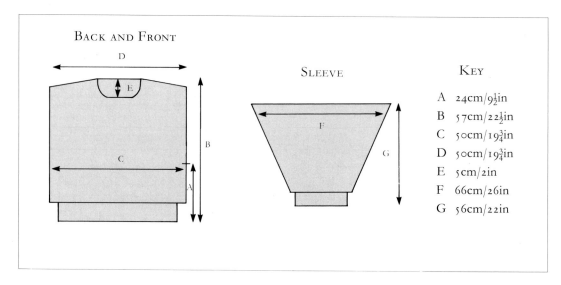

BACK AND FRONT

SLEEVE

KEY

A 24cm/9½in
B 57cm/22½in
C 50cm/19¾in
D 50cm/19¾in
E 5cm/2in
F 66cm/26in
G 56cm/22in

PATTERN CHART

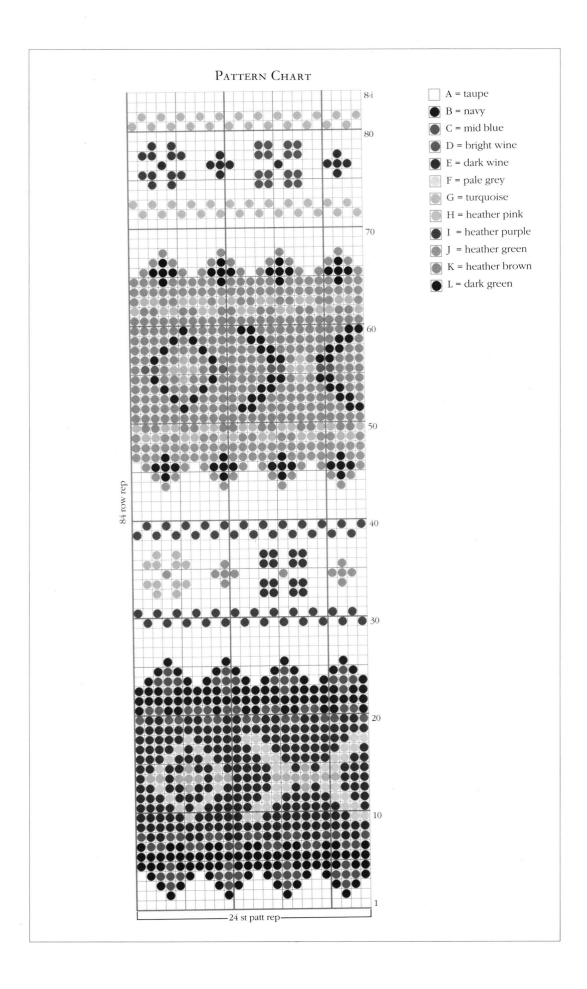

A = taupe
B = navy
C = mid blue
D = bright wine
E = dark wine
F = pale grey
G = turquoise
H = heather pink
I = heather purple
J = heather green
K = heather brown
L = dark green

HURLINGHAM

THIS MY ALL-TIME FAVOURITE FAIR ISLE PATTERN. I HAVE USED

IT OVER THE YEARS IN LOTS OF DIFFERENT WAYS, BUT I LOVE

THIS COMBINATION WITH THE CABLED BACK AND SLEEVES.

———————◆———————

MATERIALS
450g/16oz of a double knitting (US worsted weight) Shetland wool in main colour A
50g/1¾oz each in contrast colours B, C, D, E, F, G, H and I
Small amount in contrast colour J
Pair each of 3¼mm (US 3) and 4mm (US 6) knitting needles
Cable needle
5 buttons

MEASUREMENTS
Actual measurements
Bust 90cm/35½in
Length to shoulders 49cm/19¼in
Sleeve seam 47cm/18½in

TENSION/GAUGE
30 sts and 32 rows to 10cm/4in measured over cable patt worked on 4mm (US 6) needles
22 sts and 28 rows to 10cm/4in measured over Fair Isle patt worked on 4mm (US 6) needles

Please check your tension/gauge carefully and change needle size if necessary

Pattern No 1 (worked over 8 sts)
Row 1 P2, k4, p2.
Row 2 K2, p4, k2.
Row 3 P2, C4F (see page 159), p2.
Row 4 As row 2.

These 4 rows form the patt and are repeated throughout.

Pattern No 2 (worked over 12 sts)
Row 1 P2, [k1 tbl] twice, k4, [k1 tbl] twice, p2.
Rows 2, 4, 6 and 8 K2, [p1 tbl] twice, p4, [p1 tbl] twice, k2.
Row 3 P2, [k1 tbl] twice, C4B, [k1 tbl] twice, p2.
Row 5 As row 1.
Row 7 As row 1.
Row 9 P2, slip next 4 sts on to cable needle and leave at front of work, k2, then k first 2 sts on cable needle, bring cable needle to front of work, k2, then k2 from cable needle, p2.
Row 10 As row 2.
These 10 rows from the patt and are repeated throughout.

BACK
Using smaller needles and A cast on 91 sts.
Rib row 1 (RS) K3, * p1, [k1 tbl, p1] twice, k3, rep from * to end.
Rib row 2 K3, * p1, [k1 tbl, p1] twice, k3, rep from * to end.
Rows 3 to 6 Rep rows 1 and 2 twice more.
Row 7 K3, * p1, slip next 2 sts on to cable needle and leave at front, k1 tbl, then p1, k1 tbl from cable needle, p1, k3, rep from * to end.
Row 8 As row 2.

Rep these 8 rows once more, then row 1 again.

Inc row Rib 1, * M1, rib 2, rep from * to end. 136 sts.

Change to larger needles and patt.

Row 1 For moss/seed st p1, [k1, p1] 3 times, * work row 1 of pattern No 2 over next 12 sts, p1, work row 1 of pattern No 1 over next 8 sts, p1, rep from * 4 times more, work row 1 of pattern No 2 over next 12 sts, for moss/seed st p1, [k1, p1] 3 times.

Row 2 For moss/seed st p1, [k1, p1] 3 times, * work row 2 of pattern No 2 over next 12 sts, k1, work row 2 of pattern No 1 over next 8 sts, k1, rep from * 4 times more, work row 2 of pattern No 2 over next 12 sts, for moss/seed st p1, [k1, p1] 3 times.

Cont straight in patt as set until back measures 28cm/11in from cast-on edge, ending with a WS row.

Shape armholes

Cast/bind off 7 sts at beg of next 2 rows. Keeping continuity of patt dec 1 st at each end of the next and foll alt row. 118 sts. Cont straight in patt until back measures 49cm/19¼in from cast-on edge, ending with a WS row.

Shape shoulders

Cast/bind off 11 sts at beg of next 2 rows and 12 sts at the beg of the foll 4 rows.

Cast/bind off rem 48 sts.

SLEEVES

Using smaller needles and A cast on 43 sts. Work 17 rows in rib patt as given for back, ending with a RS row.

Inc row Rib 2, * M1, rib 4, M1, rib 3, rep from * to last 6 sts, [M1, rib 2] 3 times. 56 sts. Change to larger needles and patt.

Row 1 K1, p1, * work row 1 of pattern No 1 over next 8 sts, p1, work row 1 of pattern No 2 over next 12 sts, p1, rep from * once more, work row 1 of pattern No 1 over next 8 sts, p1, k1.

Row 2 P1, k1, * work row 2 of patt No 1 over next 8 sts, k1, work row 2 of patt No 2 over next 12 sts, k1, rep from * once, work row 2 of patt No 1 over 8 sts, k1, p1.

Keeping patt correct, inc and work into patt 1 st at each end of the next and every foll 5th row until there are 100 sts.

Work straight until sleeve measures 47cm/18½in from cast-on edge, ending with a WS row.

Shape top

Cast/bind off 7 sts at the beg of next 2 rows. Dec 1 st at each end of the next and every foll alt row until 52 sts rem.

Cast/bind off 2 sts at beg of next 2 rows and 3 sts at beg of foll 2 rows. 42 sts.

Next row * Work 3 tog, rep from * to end. Cast/bind off.

POCKET LININGS (make 2)

Using larger needles and A cast on 22 sts. Work 10cm/4in in st st ending with a p row. Leave sts on a spare needle.

LEFT FRONT

Using smaller needles and A cast on 43 sts. Work 17 rows in rib patt as given for back ending with a RS row.

Inc row Rib 3, * M1, rib 6, rep from * to last 4 sts, M1, rib 4. 50 sts.

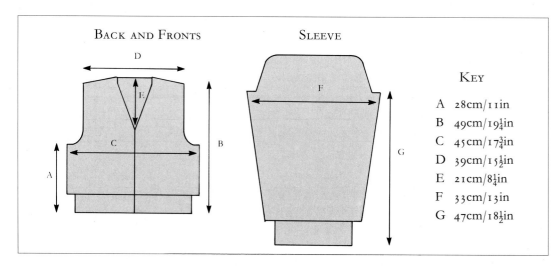

BACK AND FRONTS

SLEEVE

KEY

A 28cm/11in
B 49cm/19¼in
C 45cm/17¾in
D 39cm/15½in
E 21cm/8¼in
F 33cm/13in
G 47cm/18½in

Change to larger needles.

Work in st st in patt from chart as foll:

Row 1 (RS) Work 12 st patt rep of row 1 four times, then work first 2 sts of row 1.

Row 2 Work last 2 sts of row 2, then work 12 st patt rep of row 2 four times.

Cont in patt as set until front measures 13cm/ 5in from cast-on edge, ending with a WS row.

Place pocket

Next row Patt 14 sts, slip next 22 sts on to a holder, then k across 22 sts from one pocket lining, patt rem 14 sts.

Cont in patt as set until front measures 28cm/ 11in from cast-on edge ending with a WS row.

Shape armhole and neck

Dec 1 st at neck edge of next row and 15 foll 3rd rows *at the same time* shape armhole by casting/binding off 7 sts at beg of next row, then dec 1 st at armhole edge on the 3 foll alt rows.

Cont straight in patt until front measures the same as back to shoulder shaping ending at armhole edge.

Shape shoulder

Cast/bind off 8 sts at beg of next and foll alt row. Work 1 row.

Cast/bind off rem 8 sts.

RIGHT FRONT

Work to match left front, reversing all shapings and Fair Isle pattern.

FRONT BAND

Join shoulders.

Using smaller needles and A cast on 9 sts.

Rib row 1 K2, [p1, k1] 3 times, k1.

Row 2 K1, [p1, k1] 4 times.

Rep the last 2 rows once more.

Buttonhole row 1 Rib 4, cast/bind off 2 sts, rib to end.

Buttonhole row 2 Rib 3, cast on 2 sts, rib to end.

Work in rib for 3.5cm/1½in.

Rep the 2 buttonhole rows.

Cont in rib making 3 more buttonholes when band measures 12cm/4¾in, 19.5cm/7¾in and 27cm/10¾in from cast-on edge.

Cont in rib until band when slightly stretched fits up right front across back neck and down left front.

POCKET TOPS

With right side facing using smaller needles and A, increasing 1 st at centre, k across sts from holder. 23 sts.

Row 1 K1, * p1, k1, rep from * to end.

Row 2 P1, * k1, p1, rep from * to end.

Rep the last 2 rows once more.

Cast/bind off in rib.

FINISHING

Set in sleeves. Join side and sleeve seams. Sew pockets and row ends of pocket tops in place. Sew on front band. Sew on buttons.

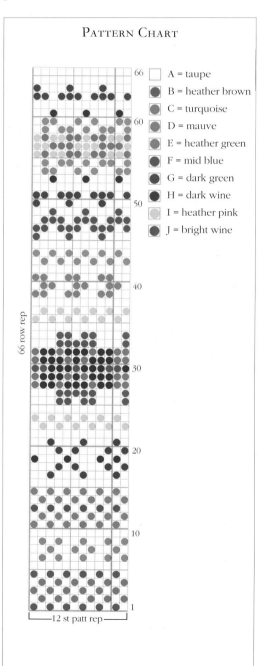

PATTERN CHART

A = taupe
B = heather brown
C = turquoise
D = mauve
E = heather green
F = mid blue
G = dark green
H = dark wine
I = heather pink
J = bright wine

66 row rep

12 st patt rep

BLOOMSBURY

USED ON ITS OWN, THIS HERRINGBONE TWEED STITCH CREATES

A BEAUTIFUL TEXTURED SWEATER. HERE I HAVE ADDED A TOUCH

OF COLOUR, INSPIRED BY AN OLD KELIM, AT THE YOKE AND CUFF.

◆

MATERIALS
450g/16oz of a double knitting (US worsted weight) wool in main colour A
50g/1¾oz each of contrast colours B, C, D, E, F and G
Pair each of 3mm (US 2) and 4mm (US 6) knitting needles

MEASUREMENTS
Actual measurements
Bust 104cm/41in
Length to shoulders 67cm/26½in
Sleeve seam 47cm/18½in

TENSION/GAUGE
22 sts and 30 rows to 10cm/4in measured over patt worked on 4mm (US 6) needles
51 rows of Fair Isle band measures 21cm/8¼in

Please check your tension/gauge carefully and change needle size if necessary

NOTE
When working from chart use separate small balls of yarn for each isolated area of colour and twist yarns together at WS of work when changing colour to avoid making a hole

BACK
Using smaller needles and A cast on 102 sts.
Rib row 1 (RS) K2, * p2, k2, rep from * to end.

Rib row 2 P2, * k2, p2, rep from * to end.
Rep these 2 rows for 11.5cm/4½in ending with rib row 2.
Inc row Rib 9, * M1, rib 7, rep from * to last 9 sts, M1, rib 9. 115 sts.
Change to larger needles and patt.
Row 1 (WS) P to end.
Row 2 K1, * k2 tog, k2, k into next st 1 row below without slipping the st off the needle, then k into the st on the needle and slip both sts off the needle together, k2, rep from * to last 2 sts, k2.
Row 3 P to end.
Row 4 K3, * k into next st 1 row below without slipping the st off the needle, then k into the st on the needle and slip both sts off the needle together, k2, k2 tog, k2, rep from * ending last rep k1.
These 4 rows form the patt.
Cont straight in patt until back measures 44.5cm/17½in from cast-on edge, ending with a WS row.
Shape armholes
Cast/bind off 6 sts at beg of next 2 rows.
Keeping to patt, dec 1 st at each end of the next and 2 foll alt rows, then dec 1 st at beg of next row. 96 sts.
Beg with a k row, change to st st and work 2 rows B, 1 row C, and 1 row D.
Then work in st st in patt from pattern chart as follows:
Row 5 (RS) Work 24 st patt rep of row 5 four times.

Row 6 Work 24 st patt rep of row 6 four times.

Cont straight in patt as set, until back measures 67cm/26½in from cast-on edge, ending with row 46 of chart.

Shape shoulders

Cast/bind off 13 sts at beg of next 4 rows, keeping to chart patt.

Work in patt across rem 44 sts and leave these sts on a spare needle.

FRONT

Work as given for back until row 24 of Fair Isle band has been worked.

Shape neck

Next row (RS) Patt 36 sts, turn and leave rem sts on a spare needle.

Dec 1 st at neck edge of next and every foll alt row until 26 sts rem.

Patt 2 rows straight so ending at armhole edge.

Shape shoulder

Cast/bind off 13 sts at beg of next row.

Work 1 row.

Cast/bind off rem 13 sts.

With right side facing return to rem sts and slip next 24 sts on to a spare needle, join on yarn, patt to end.

Dec 1 st at neck edge of next and every foll alt row until 26 sts rem.

Patt 3 rows straight so ending at armhole edge.

Shape shoulder

Cast/bind off 13 sts at beg of next row.

Work 1 row.

Cast/bind off rem 13 sts.

SLEEVES

Using smaller needles and A cast on 50 sts. Work 11.5cm/4½in rib as given for back, ending with a RS row.

Inc row Rib 2 * M1, rib 4, M1, rib 3, rep from * to last 6 sts, M1, rib 4, M1, rib 2. 64 sts.

Change to larger needles and work rows 33 to 10 from chart in st st as follows:

Row 1 (RS) Work last 8 sts of row 33, then work 24 st patt rep twice, then work first 8 sts of row 33.

Row 2 Work last 8 sts of row 32, then work 24 st patt rep twice, then work first 8 sts of row 32.

These 2 rows set the patt.

Cont in patt until row 10 has been worked.

Cut off contrast colours and cont in A.

Next row K to end.

Beg with row 1 work in patt as given for back, inc and work into patt 1 st at each end of the 3rd and every foll 6th row until there are 88 sts.

Work straight until sleeve measures 47cm/18½in from beg, ending with a WS row.

Shape top

Cast/bind off 6 sts at beg of next 2 rows.

Dec 1 st at each end of the 3 foll alt rows. 70 sts.

Row 1 Work last 11 sts of row 1, then work

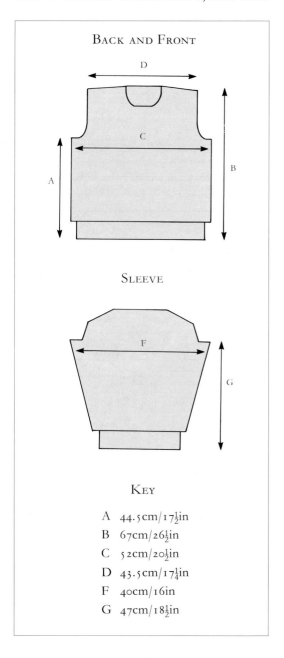

BACK AND FRONT

SLEEVE

KEY

A 44.5cm/17½in

B 67cm/26½in

C 52cm/20½in

D 43.5cm/17¼in

F 40cm/16in

G 47cm/18½in

24 st patt rep twice, then work first 11 sts of row 1.

This row sets the patt for Fair Isle band.

Keeping continuity of patt, dec 1 st at each end of the next and every foll alt row until 56 sts rem, then dec 1 st at each end of every row until 10 sts rem.

Cast/bind off.

NECKBAND

Join right shoulder seam.

With right side facing using smaller needles and A, pick up and k 19 sts down left side of front neck, 24 sts from centre front, 19 sts up right side of front neck and 44 sts from back neck. 106 sts.

Work 7 rows in rib as given for back.

Cast/bind off in rib.

FINISHING

Join left shoulder seam and neck band. Sew in sleeves. Join side and sleeve seams.

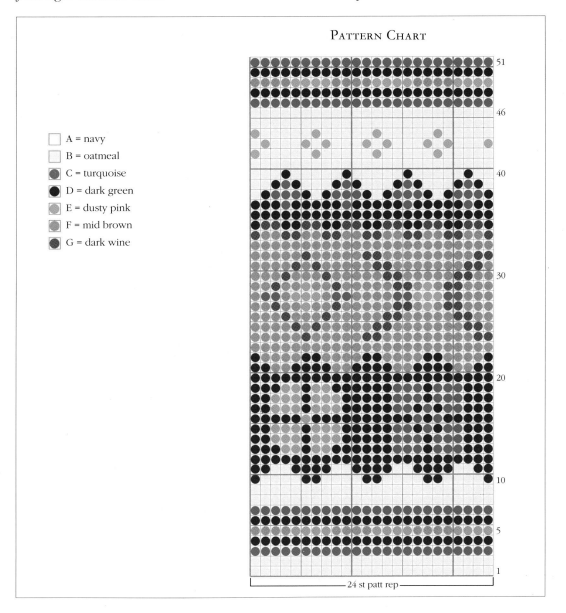

PATTERN CHART

A = navy
B = oatmeal
C = turquoise
D = dark green
E = dusty pink
F = mid brown
G = dark wine

24 st patt rep

GREENWICH

THE CLASSIC CREW IS A SWEATER THAT NO WARDROBE SHOULD

BE WITHOUT. FOR UNADULTERATED EXTRAVAGANCE, KNIT IT IN

PURE SILK AND CREATE AN HEIRLOOM FOR YOUR FUTURE

GRANDCHILDREN.

MATERIALS
450g/16oz of a lightweight soft cotton
Pair each of 2¼mm (US 1) and 4mm (US 6)
knitting needles

MEASUREMENTS
Actual measurements
Bust 96cm/38in
Length to shoulders 63.5cm/25in
Sleeve seam 52.5cm/20¾in

TENSION/GAUGE
28 sts and 40 rows to 10cm/4in measured
over patt worked on 4mm (US 6) needles

***Please check your tension/gauge carefully
and change needle size if necessary***

BACK
Using smaller needles cast on 122 sts.
Rib row 1 (RS) K2, * p2, k2, rep from * to
end.
Rib row 2 P2, * k2, p2, rep from * to end.
Rep these 2 rows for 6cm/2¼in ending with
rib row 1.
Inc row Rib 12, * M1, rib 9, rep from * to
last 11 sts, M1, rib 11. 134 sts.
Change to larger needles.
Work in patt from chart as follows:
Row 1 (RS) Work last 3 sts of row 1, then
work 32 st patt rep 4 times, then work first 3
sts of row 1.
Row 2 Work last 3 sts of row 2, then work 32

st patt rep 4 times, then work first 3 sts of
row 2.
Cont straight in patt as set, until back
measures 38cm/15in from cast-on edge,
ending with a WS row.
Shape armholes
Cast/bind off 3 sts at beg of next 2 rows.
Dec 1 st at each end of the next 3 rows.
122 sts.
Cont straight in patt until back measures
63.5cm/25in from cast-on edge, ending with
a WS row.
Shape shoulders
Cast/bind off 35 sts at beg of next 2 rows.
Leave rem 52 sts on a spare needle.

FRONT
Work as given for back until front measures
56cm/22in from beg ending with a WS row.
Shape neck
Next row Patt 51 sts, turn and leave rem sts
on a spare needle.
** Dec 1 st at neck edge on next 16 rows.
35 sts.
Cont without shaping until front measures
the same as back to shoulder ending at
armhole edge.
Shape shoulder
Cast/bind off 35 sts. **
With right side facing return to rem sts and
slip next 20 sts on to a spare needle, join on
yarn, patt to end.
Complete to match first side from ** to **.

SLEEVES

Using smaller needles cast on 46 sts.
Work 6cm/2½in rib as given for back, ending with a RS row.
Inc row Rib 2, * M1, rib 2, M1, rib 3, rep from * to last 4 sts, [M1, rib 2] twice. 64 sts.
Change to larger needles.
Work in patt from chart as follows:
Row 1 Work 32 st patt of row 13 twice.
Row 2 Work 32 st patt of row 14 twice.
These 2 rows set the patt.
Cont in patt, increase and work into patt 1 st at each end of the next and every foll 5th row until there are 134 sts.
Work straight in patt until sleeve measures 52.5cm/20¾in from cast-on edge, ending with row 42.
Cast/bind off.

NECKBAND

Join right shoulder seam.
With right side facing using smaller needles, pick up and k 25 sts down left side of front neck, 20 sts from centre front, 25 sts up right side of front neck and 52 sts from back neck. 122 sts.
Work 7 rows in rib as given for back.
Cast/bind off in rib.

FINISHING

Join left shoulder seam and neckband. Sew in sleeves. Join side and sleeve seams.

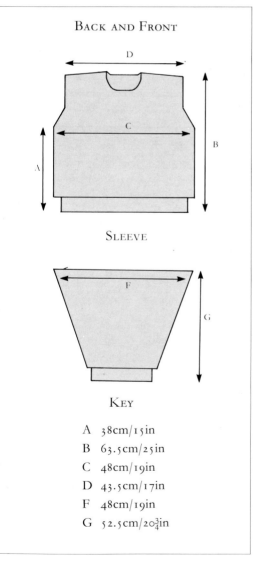

BACK AND FRONT

SLEEVE

KEY

A 38cm/15in
B 63.5cm/25in
C 48cm/19in
D 43.5cm/17in
F 48cm/19in
G 52.5cm/20¾in

Pattern Chart

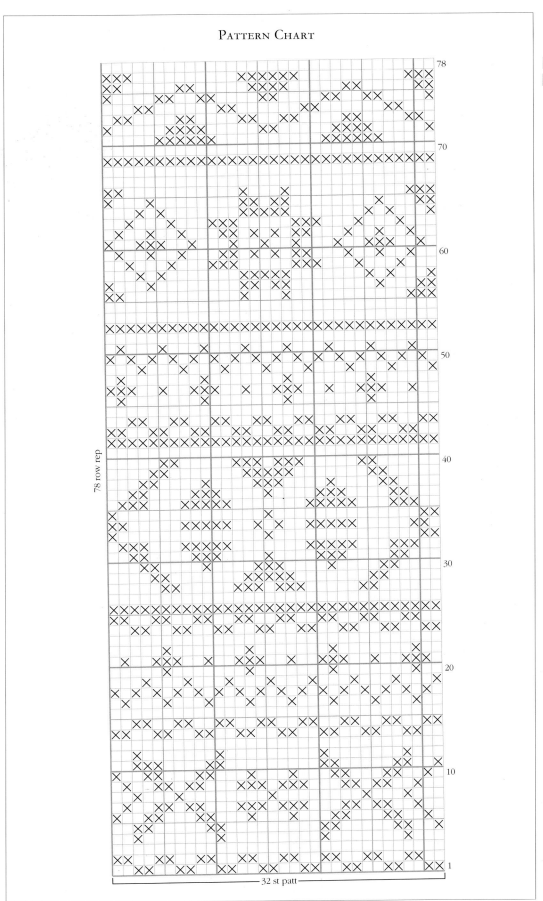

K on right side and p on wrong side

P on right side and k on wrong side

78 row rep

32 st patt

CITY

———————————— ◆ ————————————

My nine sweater designs in this chapter seem to me to be just right for a sophisticated city setting, be it Manhattan, Berlin or Venice. With each garment I have put together the appropriate stitchwork, styling and yarns to take you through a long and varied day of city living. I hope the end results are sweaters that you will find comfortable as well as elegant.

BOSTON

I ADORE CABLES AND TRELLISES AND HAVE USED BOTH

IN THIS DESIGN. I WANTED TO PAINT A MONOTONE PICTURE,

USING THE TRELLIS AS A FRAMEWORK FOR THE RANDOM

SCULPTURED STITCHWORK.

―――――――――◆―――――――――

MATERIALS
250g/9oz of a 4 ply (US sport weight) botany wool
Pair each of 2¼mm (US 1) and 3¼mm (US 3) knitting needles
Cable needle
5 buttons

MEASUREMENTS
Actual measurements
Bust 90cm/35½in
Length to shoulders 44.5cm/17½in

TENSION/GAUGE
30 sts and 40 rows to 10cm/4in measured over patt worked on 3¼mm (US 3) needles

Please check your tension/gauge carefully and change needle size if necessary

BACK
Using smaller needles cast on 110 sts.
Rib row 1 (RS) * K1, p1, rep from * to end.
Rep this row for 2cm/¾in.
Change to larger needles.
Starting at row 13 work in patt from chart, shaping sides of back as shown, until row 96 has been worked.
Shape armholes
Cast/bind off 8 sts at beg of next 2 rows.
Dec 1 st each end of the next 6 rows. 108 sts.
Cont straight in patt until row 182 has been worked.

Shape shoulders
Cast/bind off 10 sts at beg of next 4 rows and 11 sts at the beg of the foll 2 rows.
Cast/bind off rem 46 sts.

LEFT FRONT
Using larger needles cast on 2 sts.
Starting at row 1 work from chart, shaping lower edge and side as shown, until row 96 has been worked.
Shape armhole and neck
Next row (RS) Cast/bind off 8 sts, patt to last 2 sts, work 2 tog.
Cont to work from chart, shaping neck and armhole as shown. 31 sts.
Cont straight until row 182 has been worked.
Shape shoulder
Cast/bind off 10 sts at beg of next and foll alt row. Work 1 row.
Cast/bind off rem 11 sts.

RIGHT FRONT
Using larger needles cast on 2 sts.
Starting at row 1 work from chart, shaping lower edge and side as shown, until row 96 has been worked.
Shape armhole and neck
Next row Work 2 tog, patt to end.
Next row (WS) Cast/bind off 8 sts, patt to end.
Cont to work from chart, shaping neck and armhole as shown. 31 sts.

Cont straight until row 183 has been worked.

Shape shoulder

Cast/bind off 10 sts at beg of next and foll alt row.

Cast/bind off rem 11 sts.

ARMBANDS

Join shoulder seams.

With right side facing using smaller needles, pick up and k 166 sts evenly around armhole edge.

Work 2cm/¾in k1, p1 rib.

Cast/bind off in rib.

FRONT BAND

Using smaller needles cast on 10 sts.

Rib row 1 (Rs) * K1, p1, rep from * to last 2 sts, k2.

Rib row 2 * K1, p1, rep from * to end.

Rep these 2 rows until band when slightly stretched fits along lower edge of left front from side edge to first corner (at 2-st cast on), ending with a WS row.

Shape band

Cast/bind off 3 sts at beg of next and 2 foll alt rows. 1 st rems.

Slip this st back on to left hand needle and cast on 3 sts at beg of next and 2 foll alt rows. 10 sts.

Cont in rib until band when slightly stretched fits from first corner to second corner.

Shape the band as before.

Cont in rib until band when slightly stretched fits up left front across back neck and down sloping edge of right front to beg of neck shaping.

Sew band in place.

Sew on buttons to left front, the first to come 1.5cm/½in from lower edge, the fifth level with first row of neck shaping and the remaining three spaced evenly between.

Cont band, working buttonholes to correspond with buttons as follows:

Buttonhole row 1 Rib 4, cast/bind off 2 sts, rib to end.

Buttonhole row 2 Rib 4, cast on 2 sts, rib to end.

Cont in rib, shaping band to correspond with corners, until band reaches side edge of right front. Cast/bind off.

Join shaped edges in band then stitch remainder of band in place.

Join side seams.

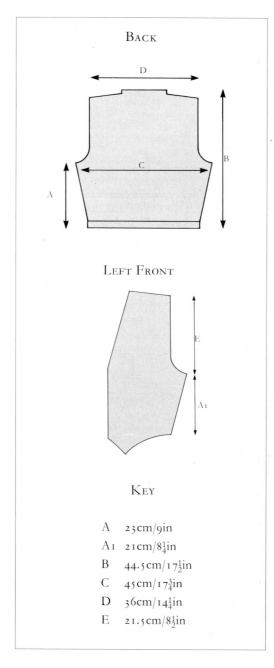

BACK

LEFT FRONT

KEY

A   23cm/9in

A1 21cm/8¼in

B   44.5cm/17½in

C   45cm/17¾in

D   36cm/14¼in

E   21.5cm/8½in

☐	K on right side and p on wrong side
☒	P on right side and k on wrong side
⟋⟋	Tw2R
⟍⟍	Tw2L
⟍⟍⟍⟍	C4F (cable — see page 159)

BACK AND FRONTS

122=19"

182
180

170

160

150

140

130

120

110

100

96

90

80

70

60

110.
8
102

50

40

122

30

20

13 Start back here

−10

−5

Start right front here

−1

Start left front here

MANHATTAN

BY COMBINING INTRICATE STITCHWORK WITH FINE YARN,

I ATTEMPTED HERE TO CREATE A TIMELESS SWEATER WHICH,

LIKE ALL THE OLD CLASSICS, WILL GET BETTER OVER THE YEARS.

MATERIALS

400g/14oz of a 4 ply (US sport weight) botany wool in main colour A

50g/1¾oz each of contrast colours B and C

Pair each of 2¼mm (US 1) and 3¼mm (US 3) knitting needles

Set of double pointed 2¼mm (US 1) needles

Cable needle

2 small buttons

MEASUREMENTS

Actual measurements

Bust 94cm/37in

Length to shoulders 57cm/22½in

Sleeve seam 44.5cm/17½in

TENSION/GAUGE

36 sts and 42 rows to 10cm/4in measured over patt worked on 3¼mm (US 3) needles

Please check your tension/gauge carefully and change needle size if necessary

NOTE

When working from chart use separate small balls of yarn for each isolated area of colour and twist yarns together at WS of work when changing colour to avoid making a hole.

BACK AND FRONT (alike)

Using smaller needles and A, cast on 141 sts.

Rib row 1 (WS) K1, * p6, k1, rep from * to end of row.

Rib row 2 P1, * k2, sl 2 purlwise, k2, p1, rep from * to end.

Rib row 3 K1, * p2, sl 2 purlwise, p2, k1, rep from * to end.

Rib row 4 P1, * slip next 2 sts on to cable needle and leave at back of work, k1, k2 from cable needle, slip next st on to cable needle and leave at front of work, k2, k1 from cable needle, p1, rep from * to end.

Rep these 4 rows for 6cm/2½in ending with rib row 1.

Inc row K3, * M1, k5, rep from * to last 3 sts, M1, k3. 169 sts.

P 1 row.

Change to larger needles.

Work in patt from chart as follows:

Row 1 (RS) Work last 35 sts of row 1, then work 37 st patt rep 3 times, then work first 23 sts of row 1.

Row 2 Work last 23 sts of row 2, then work 37 st patt rep 3 times, then work first 35 sts of row 2.

Cont straight in patt as set until work measures 34 cm/13½in from cast-on edge, ending with a WS row.

Shape armholes

Cast/bind off 6 sts at beg of next 2 rows.

Dec 1 st at each end of the next 10 rows. 137 sts.

Cont straight in patt until work measures 54cm/21¼in from cast-on edge, ending with a WS row.

Shape neck

next and every foll 4th row until there are 159 sts.

Work 7 rows straight.

Shape sleeve top

Cast/bind off 6 sts at beg of next 2 rows and 3 sts at beg of foll 2 rows.

Dec 1 st at both ends of the next 53 rows.

Cast/bind off rem 35 sts.

NECKBAND

Join shoulder seams.

With right side facing, using 3 of the double pointed needles, pick up and k 40 sts across centre front neck, 22 sts up right side of front

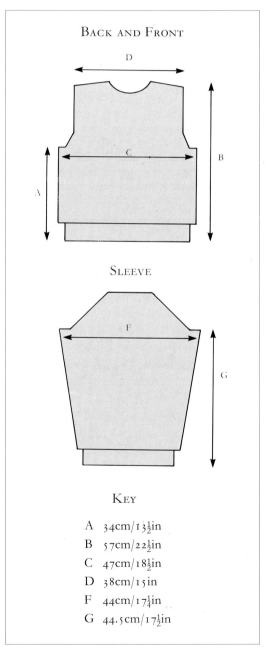

Next row Patt 54 sts, turn and leave rem sts on a spare needle.

** Dec 1 st at neck edge on the next 9 rows. 45 sts.

Shape shoulder

Next row Cast/bind off 14 sts, patt to last 2 sts, work 2 tog.

Next row Work 2 tog, patt to end.

Rep the last 2 rows once more.

Cast/bind off rem 13 sts. **

With right side facing, join yarn to rem sts, cast/bind off 29 sts, patt to end.

Complete to match first side from ** to **.

SLEEVES

Using smaller needles and A cast on 64 sts.

Work 6cm/2½in rib as given for back, ending with rib row 1.

Inc row K5, * M1, k3, rep from * to last 5 sts, M1, k5. 83 sts.

Change to larger needles and work from chart as follows:

Row 1 (RS) Work last 29 sts of row 17, then work 37 st patt rep once, then work first 17 sts of row 17.

Row 2 Work last 17 sts of row 18, then work 37 st patt rep once, then work first 29 sts of row 18.

Cont in patt as set, inc 1 st each end of the

BACK AND FRONT

SLEEVE

KEY

A   34cm/13½in
B   57cm/22½in
C   47cm/18½in
D   38cm/15in
F   44cm/17¼in
G   44.5cm/17½in

neck, 22 sts down right side of back neck, 40 sts across centre back neck, 22 sts up left side of back neck, 22 sts down left side of front neck, turn and cast on 8 sts. 176 sts.
Work 5 rows rib patt as given for back.
Buttonhole row 1 (RS) Patt 6 sts, cast/bind off 3 sts, patt to end.
Buttonhole row 2 Patt to end, casting on 3 sts over the 3 sts cast/bound off in the previous row.

Patt 6 more rows.
Rep the 2 buttonhole rows.
Patt 3 more rows.
Cast/bind off.

FINISHING
Sew 8 cast-on sts of collar to neck edge behind collar for button border. Sew on buttons. Set in sleeves, easing in fullness at top. Join side and sleeve seams.

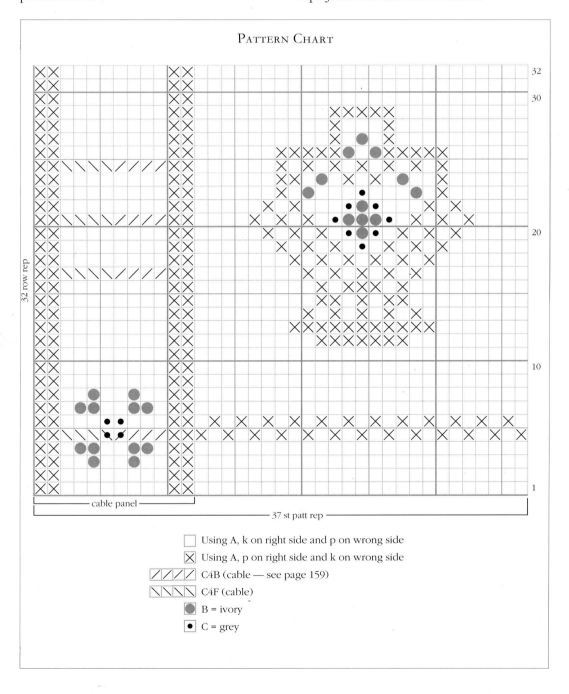

PATTERN CHART

cable panel

37 st patt rep

32 row rep

☐ Using A, k on right side and p on wrong side
☒ Using A, p on right side and k on wrong side
⟋⟋⟋⟋ C4B (cable — see page 159)
⟍⟍⟍⟍ C4F (cable)
● B = ivory
• C = grey

YORK

My source for this sweater was Art Deco fans. The fan shape is echoed in the scalloped ribbing and the collar tipped with a softly-ruffled lacy stitch.

———————◆———————

MATERIALS
350g/12½oz of a 4 ply (US sport weight) botany wool in main colour A
50g/1¾oz each of contrast colours B, C, D, E, F and G
Pair each of 2¼mm (US 1) and 3mm (US 3) knitting needles
Cable needle

MEASUREMENTS
Actual measurements
Bust 105cm/41½in
Length to shoulders 59cm/23½in
Sleeve seam 44.5cm/17½in

TENSION/GAUGE
32 sts and 38 rows to 10cm/4in measured over patt worked on 3mm (US 3) needles

Please check your tension/gauge carefully and change needle size if necessary

NOTE
When working from chart use separate small balls of yarn for each isolated area of colour and twist yarns together at WS of work when changing colour to avoid making a hole.

BACK
Using smaller needles and A, cast on 148 sts.
Rib row (RS) * K1, p1, rep from * to end.
Rep this row 19 times more. Work in patt from chart as follows:

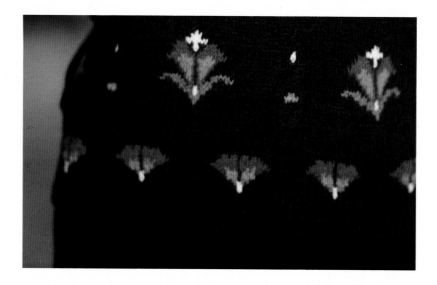

Row 21 (RS) Work last 22 sts of row 21, then work 52 st patt rep twice, then work first 22 sts of row 21.

Row 22 Work last 22 sts of row 22, then work 52 st patt rep twice, then work first 22 sts of row 22.

Cont in patt as set for 8 rows more.

Change to larger needles.

Cont straight in patt for 4 rows.

Inc and work into patt 1 st each end of the next and every foll 10th row until there are 168 sts, *at the same time* work to end of row 116, then begin patt again on row 45. (Rows 45 to 116 form the patt).

Cont straight until back measures 38cm/15in from cast-on edge, ending with a WS row.

Shape armholes

Cast/bind off 6 sts at beg of next 2 rows.

Dec 1 st each end of the next 9 rows. 138 sts.

Cont straight in patt until back measures 59 cm/23½in from cast-on edge, ending with a WS row.

Shape shoulders

Cast/bind off 14 sts at beg of next 4 rows and 13 sts at the beg of the foll 2 rows.

Cast/bind off rem 56 sts.

FRONT

Work as given for back until front measures 52cm/20½in from beg ending with a WS row.

Shape neck

Next row Patt 61 sts, turn and leave rem sts on a spare needle.

** Dec 1 st at neck edge on next 20 rows. 41 sts.

Cont straight until front measures same as back to shoulder ending at armhole edge.

Shape shoulder

Cast/bind off 14 sts at beg of next and foll alt row.

Work 1 row. Cast/bind off rem 13 sts. **

With right side facing, join yarn to rem sts, cast/bind off next 16 sts, patt to end.

Complete to match first side from ** to **.

SLEEVES

Using smaller needles and A, cast on 62 sts.

Work 6cm/2½in rib as given for back, ending with a RS row.

Inc row Rib 2, * M1, rib 3, rep from * to end. 82 sts.

Change to larger needles and starting on row 71, work from chart as follows:

Row 1 (RS) Work last 15 sts of row 71, then work 52 st patt once, then work first 15 sts of row 71.

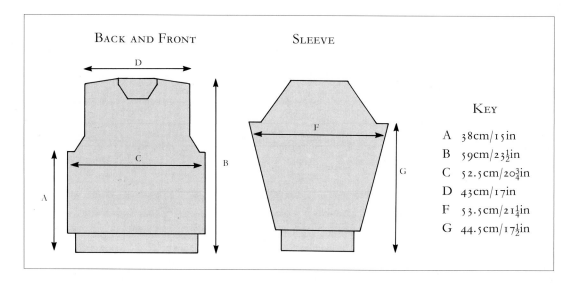

BACK AND FRONT   SLEEVE

KEY

A 38cm/15in
B 59cm/23½in
C 52.5cm/20¾in
D 43cm/17in
F 53.5cm/21¼in
G 44.5cm/17½in

Row 2 Work last 15 sts of row 72, then work 52 st patt rep once, then work first 15 sts of row 72.

Cont in patt as set, inc 1 st at each end of the 3rd and every foll 4th row until there are 150 sts.

Cont straight until sleeve measures 44.5cm/ 17½in from cast-on edge, ending with a WS row.

Shape sleeve top

Cast/bind off 6 sts at beg of next 2 rows.

Dec 1 st at each end of the next 52 rows.

Cast/bind off rem 34 sts.

COLLAR

Using smaller needles and A, cast on 123 sts.

Row 1 (RS) K1, sl 1, * k1, p1, rep from * to last 3 sts, k1, sl 1, k1.

Row 2 K1, * p1, k1, rep from * to end.

Rep these 2 rows until collar measures 5cm/ 2in from cast-on edge, ending with a RS row.

Next row * (Insert right hand needle knitwise into next st, keeping st on left hand needle draw a loop through it, slip new loop on right hand needle on to left hand needle) twice, then cast/bind off 3 sts, place st from right hand needle back on to left needle, rep from * to end.

Fasten off.

FINISHING

Join shoulder seams. Set in sleeves, easing in fullness at top. Join side and sleeve seams.

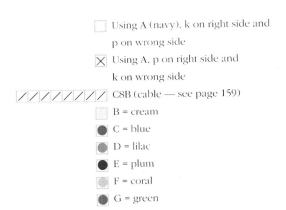

☐ Using A (navy), k on right side and
p on wrong side

☒ Using A, p on right side and
k on wrong side

⟋⟋⟋⟋⟋⟋⟋⟋ C8B (cable — see page 159)

☐ B = cream

● C = blue

● D = lilac

● E = plum

● F = coral

● G = green

PATTERN CHART

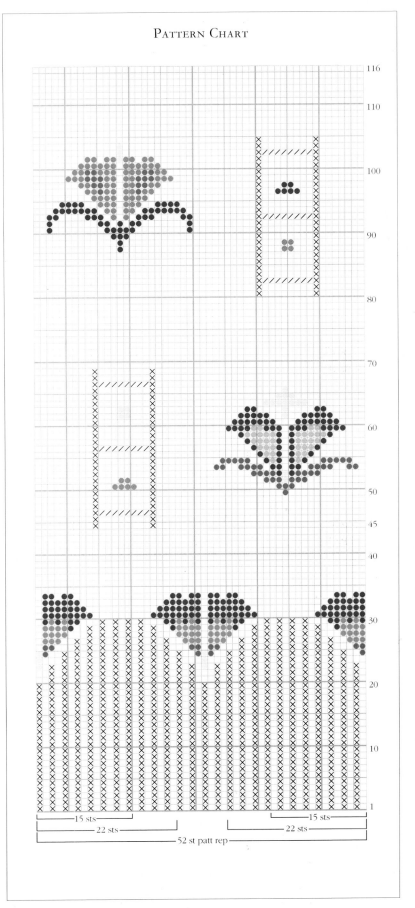

VIENNA

THERE'S A LOT OF THIRTIES INFLUENCE IN STYLING HERE.

I HAVE USED THE VERTICAL COTTON CABLES TO ACCENTUATE

THE ELEGANT LINES OF THE SWEATER.

———————◆———————

MATERIALS
450g/16oz of a medium weight cotton or
cotton/linen mixture
Pair each of 3mm (US 2) and 4mm (US 6)
knitting needles
Set of double pointed 3mm (US 2) needles
Cable needle
2 buttons

MEASUREMENTS
Actual measurements
Bust 92cm/36in
Length to shoulders 57cm/22½in

TENSION/GAUGE
29 sts and 32 rows to 10cm/4in measured
over patt worked on 4mm (US 6) needles

*Please check your tension/gauge carefully
and change needle size if necessary*

Pattern No 1 (worked over 20 sts)
Row 1 P2, k2, p4, k4, p4, k2, p2.
Row 2 and every alt row K the k sts and p
the p sts as they show.
Row 3 P2, k2, p4, C4B (see page 159), p4, k2,
p2.
Row 5 P2, Cr3L, p2, Cr3R, Cr3L, p2, Cr3R,
p2.
Row 7 P3, Cr3L, Cr3R, p2, Cr3L, Cr3R, p3.
Row 9 P4, C2B, p4, C2B, p4.
Row 11 [P4, k4] twice, p4.
Row 13 As row 9.

Row 15 P3, Cr3R, Cr3L, p2, Cr3R, Cr3L,
p3.
Row 17 P2, Cr3R, p2, Cr3L, Cr3R, p2,
Cr3L, p2.
Row 19 As row 3.
Row 20 As row 2.
These 20 rows form the patt.

Pattern No 2 (worked over 14 sts)
Row 1 P4, k6, p4.
Row 2 K4, p6, k4.
Row 3 P4, C6B, p4.
Rows 4, 6, 8 and 10 K4, p6, k4.
Rows 5 and 7 As row 1.
Row 9 As row 3.
Row 11 P3, Cr4R, Cr4L, p3.
Rows 12, 14, 16, 18, 20, 22 and 24 K3, p3,
k2, p3, k3.
Rows 13, 15, 17, 19, 21 and 23 P3, k3, p2,
k3, p3.
Row 25 P3, Cr4L, Cr4R, p3.
Row 26 As row 4.
Rows 3 to 26 form the patt.

Pattern No 3 (worked over 18sts)
Row 1 P6, k6, p6.
Row 2 K6, p6, k6.
Row 3 P6, k2, C4F, p6.
Row 4 and every foll alt row K the k sts and
p the p sts as they show.
Row 5 P6, C4B, k2, p6.
Row 7 P6, k2, C4F, p6.
Row 9 P6, C4B, k2, p6.

Row 11 P6, k2, C4F, p6.
Row 13 P6, C4B, k2, p6.
Row 15 P5, Cr3R, k2, Cr3L, p5.
Row 17 P4, Cr3R, p1, k2, p1, Cr3L, p4.
Row 19 P3, Cr3R, p2, k2, p2, Cr3L, p3.
Row 21 P3, Cr3L, p2, k2, p2, Cr3R, p3.
Row 23 P4, Cr3L, p1, k2, p1, Cr3R, p4.
Row 25 P5, Cr3L, k2, Cr3R, p5.
Row 26 K6, p6, k6.
Rows 3 to 26 form the patt.

BACK
Using smaller needles cast on 114 sts.
Rib row 1 (RS) K2, * p2, k2, rep from * to end.
Rib row 2 P2, * k2, p2, rep from * to end.
Rep these 2 rows for 15cm/6in ending with rib row 1.
Inc row Rib 4, * M1, rib 6, M1, rib 5, rep from * to end. 134 sts.
Change to larger needles.
Work in patt as follows:
Row 1 P7, k1, work row 1 of patt No 2, k1, work row 1 of patt No 3, k1, work row 1 of patt No 2, k1, work row 1 of patt No 1, k1, work row 1 of patt No 2, k1, work row 1 of patt No 3, k1, work row 1 of patt No 2, k1, p7.
Row 2 P8, work row 2 of patt No 2, p1, work row 2 of patt No 3, p1, work row 2 of patt No 2, p1, work row 2 of patt No 1, p1, work row 2 of patt No 2, p1, work row 2 of patt No 3, p1, work row 2 of patt No 2, p8.
Cont straight in patt as set until back measures 35.5cm/14in from cast-on edge, ending with a WS row.
Mark each end of last row with a coloured thread.
Cont straight in patt until back measures 53cm/21in from cast-on edge, ending with a WS row.
Dec row K2, * k2 tog, k2, rep from * to end. 101 sts.
Patt row K1, * p1, k1, rep from * to end.
Rep this row until back measures 57cm/22½in from cast-on edge, ending with a WS row.
Shape shoulders and back neck
Patt 33 sts, turn and leave rem sts on a spare needle, patt to end.
Cast/bind off 5 sts at beg of next and 4 foll alt rows. Work 1 row. Cast/bind off rem 8 sts.

With right side facing slip next 35 sts of rem sts on to a spare needle, join on yarn, patt to end.
Cast/bind off 5 sts at beg of next and 4 foll alt rows. Work 1 row. Cast/bind off rem 8 sts.

FRONT
Work as given for back until front measures 38cm/15in from beg ending with a WS row.
Shape neck
Next row Patt 67 sts, turn and leave rem sts on a spare needle.
** Dec 1 st at neck edge on next and every foll alt row until 44 sts rem.
Cont straight in patt until front measures 53cm/21in from cast-on edge, ending with a WS row.
Dec row K1, * k2 tog, k2, rep from * to last 3 sts, k2 tog, k1. 33 sts.
Patt row K1, * p1, k1, rep from * to end.
Rep this row until back measures 57cm/22½in from cast-on edge, ending at armhole edge.
Shape shoulder
Cast/bind off 5 sts at beg of next and 4 foll alt rows. Work 1 row.
Cast/bind off rem 8 sts. **

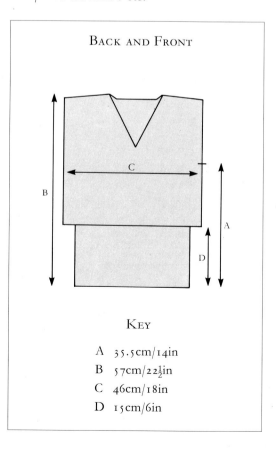

BACK AND FRONT

KEY

A 35.5cm/14in
B 57cm/22½in
C 46cm/18in
D 15cm/6in

With right side facing, join yarn to rem sts and patt to end.
Complete to match first side from ** to **.

NECKBAND

Join shoulder seams. With right side facing, using the set of needles, pick up and k 60 sts up right side of front neck, 6 sts down right side of back neck, work in moss/seed st across 35 sts at centre back, pick up and k 6 sts up left side of back neck and 60 sts down left side of front neck. 167 sts.
Work 3 rows moss/seed st.
Work first buttonhole on next row as foll:
Buttonhole row 1 Moss/seed st 4 sts, cast/bind off 3 sts, moss/seed st to end.
Buttonhole row 2 Work in moss/seed st casting on 3 sts over those cast/bound off in previous row.
Work 4 rows moss/seed st.
Rep the 2 buttonhole rows.
Work 2 rows moss/seed st.
Cast/bind off.

ARMBANDS

With right side facing, using smaller needles pick up and k 134 sts between coloured threads.
Work 2 rows rib as given on back.
Cast/bind off in rib.

FINISHING

Join side and armband seams. Sew on buttons.

CANTERBURY

HERE IS A CHUNKY BOLERO WITH A SPICY FLAVOUR IN

COLOUR AND STYLING. THE MOSS STITCH CREATES A TEXTURED

GRAINY BACKGROUND FOR THE MORE INTENSE, HOT COLOURS

OF THE DIAMONDS.

MATERIALS

550g/19½oz of an Aran weight wool in main colour A

50g/1¾oz each of contrast colours B, C, and D

25g/1oz of contrast colour E

Pair each of 4mm (US 6) and 5mm (US 8) knitting needles

1 spare 4mm (US 6) needle

2 buttons

MEASUREMENTS

Actual measurements

Across back below armhole 47cm/18½in

Length to shoulders 37cm/14½in

Sleeve seam 48cm/19in

TENSION/GAUGE

17 sts and 28 rows to 10cm/4in measured over patt worked on 5mm (US 8) needles

Please check your tension/gauge carefully and change needle size if necessary

NOTE

When working from chart use separate small balls of yarn for each isolated area of colour and twist yarns together at WS of work when changing colour to avoid making a hole.

Moss/seed st patt (shown as blank square on chart)

Worked over an odd No of sts:

Patt row K1, * p1, k1, rep from * to end.

This row forms the patt.

Worked over an even No of sts:

Row 1 * K1, p1, rep from * to end.

Row 2 * P1, k1, rep from * to end.

These 2 rows form the patt.

Bobble

To make a bobble, work to the position shown for bobble, then using correct colour, knit into the stitch below the next st on left hand needle, replace this st on left hand needle and k into front, back and front again (3 sts), turn, p3, then lift 2nd and third sts over first and off the needle, turn, k2 tog. This completes the bobble.

BACK

Using smaller needles and A cast on 79 sts.

Rib row 1 (RS) K1, * p1, k1, rep from * to end.

Rib row 2 P1, * k1, p1, rep from * to end.

Rep these 2 rows for 4.5cm/1¾in ending with rib row 2 and inc 1 st at end of last row. 80 sts.

Change to larger needles.

Work in patt from chart to end of row 30.

Shape armholes

Cast/bind off 5 sts at beg of next 2 rows. 60 sts.

Cont straight in patt until row 92 has been completed.

Cast/bind off in patt.

Cast/bind off in patt.

RIGHT FRONT
Using smaller needles and A cast on 29 sts.
Rib row 1 (RS) K1, * p1, k1, rep from * to end.
Rib row 2 P1, * k1, p1, rep from * to end.
Rep these 2 rows for 4.5cm/1¾in ending with rib row 2.
Change to larger needles.
Work in patt from chart to end of row 31.
Shape armhole
Next row Cast/bind off 5 sts, patt to end. 24 sts.
Cont in patt until row 44 has been worked.
Place pocket
Next row Patt 2 sts, place next 21 sts on a holder, work in patt across 21 sts of one pocket lining, patt rem 1 st.
Cont in patt until row 92 has been worked.
Cast/bind off in patt.

POCKET LININGS (make 2)
Using larger needles and A cast on 21 sts.
Work 24 rows in st st. Leave these sts on a spare needle.

LEFT FRONT
Using smaller needles and A cast on 29 sts.
Rib row 1 (RS) K1, * p1, k1, rep from * to end.
Rib row 2 P1, * k1, p1, rep from * to end.
Rep these 2 rows for 4.5cm/1¾in ending with rib row 2.
Change to larger needles.
Work in patt from chart to end of row 30.
Shape armhole
Next row Cast/bind off 5 sts, patt to end. 24 sts.
Cont in patt until row 44 has been worked.
Place pocket
Next row Patt 1 st, place next 21 sts on a holder, work in patt across 21 sts of one pocket lining, patt rem 2 sts.
Cont in patt until row 92 has been worked.

SLEEVES
Using smaller needles and A cast on 39 sts.
Work 9cm/3½in rib as given for back, ending with a WS row and inc 1 st at end of last row. 40 sts.
Change to larger needles and work 6 rows in moss/seed st, increasing 1 st at each end of the 3rd row. 42 sts.
Row 7 Moss/seed st 7 sts, * using any contrast colour, k into front, back and front again of next st, turn, p3, then lift 2nd and third sts over first and off the needle, turn, break off contrast yarn, moss/seed st 6 sts, rep from * to end.
Cont in moss/seed st, increasing 1 st each end of every 10th row until there are 60 sts.
Continue straight until sleeve measures

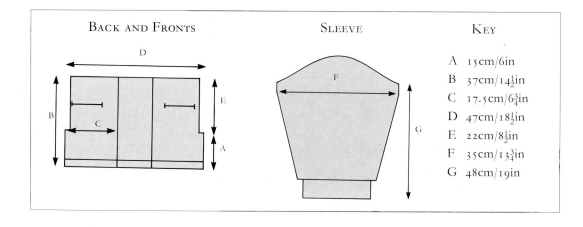

BACK AND FRONTS	SLEEVE	KEY
		A 15cm/6in
		B 37cm/14½in
		C 17.5cm/6¾in
		D 47cm/18½in
		E 22cm/8½in
		F 35cm/13¾in
		G 48cm/19in

48cm/19in from cast-on edge, ending with a WS row.

Shape top

Cast/bind off 5 sts at beg of next 2 rows. Dec 1 st each end of the next and every foll alt row until 18 sts rem. Cast/bind off.

POCKET TOPS

With right side facing, using smaller needles and A, rib 9, cast/bind off next 2 sts, rib 9.

Next row Rib 10, cast on 2 sts, rib 9. Rib 4 more rows. Cast/bind off in rib.

FRONT BAND

Join shoulder seams.

Using an extra smaller needle and A, beg at cast-on edge and pick up and k 94 sts up right front, 23 sts across back neck and 94 sts down left front.

Work 6 rows rib. Cast/bind off in rib.

FINISHING

Set in sleeves. Join side and sleeve seams. Sew buttons to pocket lining to correspond with buttonholes.

BACK AND FRONTS

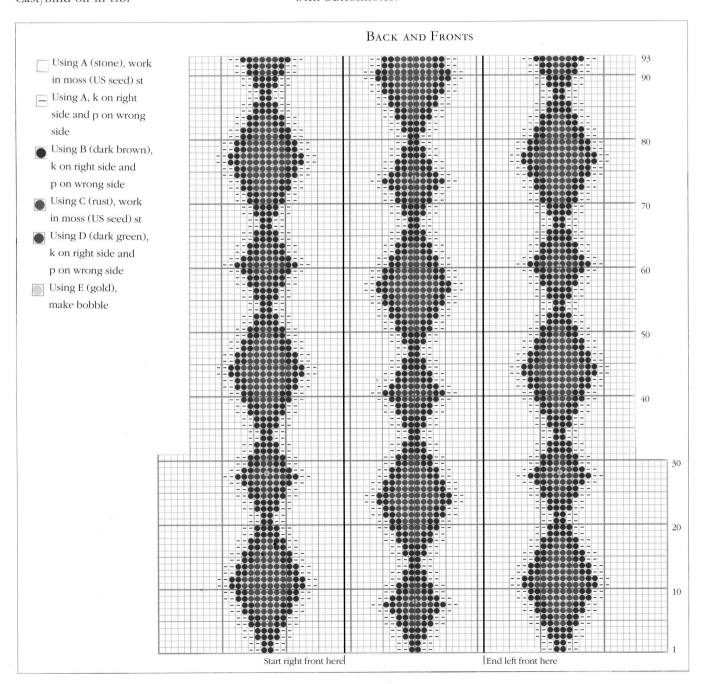

Using A (stone), work in moss (US seed) st

Using A, k on right side and p on wrong side

Using B (dark brown), k on right side and p on wrong side

Using C (rust), work in moss (US seed) st

Using D (dark green), k on right side and p on wrong side

Using E (gold), make bobble

Start right front here

End left front here

CASABLANCA

THERE IS A LOT OF NOSTALGIA IN THIS SWEATER WITH ITS

PRETTY OLD-FASHIONED FLOWERS AND ITS ANTIQUE, DUSTY

COLOURS ON AN IVORY GROUND — DEFINITELY A MUST FOR

ANY FOREIGN ASSIGNMENT.

MATERIALS
550g/19½oz of a lightweight soft cotton in main colour A
50g/1¾oz each of contrast colours B, C, D and E
Pair each of 2¼mm (US 1) and 3¼mm (US 3) knitting needles
Set of double pointed 2¼mm (US 1) needles

MEASUREMENTS
Actual measurements
Bust 96cm/38in
Length to shoulders 62cm/24½in
Sleeve seam 56cm/22in

TENSION/GAUGE
28 sts and 36 rows to 10cm/4in measured over patt worked on 3¼mm (US 3) needles

Please check your tension/gauge carefully and change needle size if necessary

NOTE
When working from charts use separate small balls of yarn for each isolated area of colour and twist yarns together at WS of work when changing colour to avoid making a hole.

BACK
Using smaller needles and A cast on 118 sts.
Rib row 1 (RS) K2, * p2, k2, rep from * to end.
Rib row 2 P2, * k2, p2, rep from * to end.

Rep these 2 rows for 6cm/2½in ending with rib row 1.
Inc row Rib 6, * M1, rib 7, rep from * to end. 134 sts.
Change to larger needles.
Work in patt from chart, beg with row 1 until row 112 has been worked.
Shape armholes
Cast/bind off 3 sts at beg of next 2 rows. Dec 1 st at each end of the next 3 rows. 122 sts.
Cont straight in patt until row 202 has been worked.
Shape shoulders
Cast/bind off 35 sts, k until there are 52 sts on needle, cast/bind off rem 35 sts.

FRONT
Work as given for back until row 175 has been worked.
Shape neck
Next row (WS) Patt 51 sts, turn and leave rem sts on a spare needle.
Dec 1 st at neck edge on next 16 rows.
Cont straight until row 202 is reached.
Cast/bind off.
With wrong side facing slip next 20 sts on to a spare needle, join on yarn, patt to end.
Dec 1 st at neck edge on next 16 rows.
Cont straight until row 202 is reached.
Cast/bind off.

SLEEVES
Using smaller needles and A cast on 46 sts.

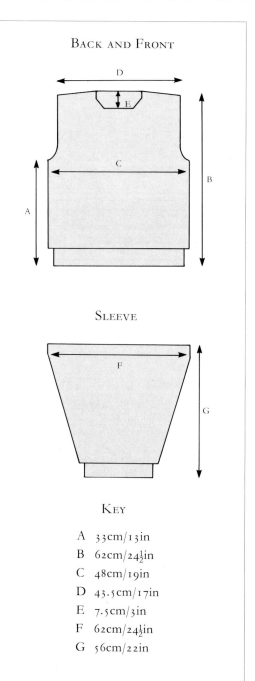

Work 6cm/2½in rib as given for back, ending with a RS row.

Inc row Rib 2, * M1, rib 2, rep from * to end. 68 sts.

Change to larger needles and work from chart, shaping sides of sleeves as shown, until row 181 has been worked

Cast/bind off.

NECKBAND

Join shoulder seams. Using 3 needles from the set, pick up and k 24 sts down left side of front neck, k across 20 sts at centre front, pick up and k 24 sts up right side of front neck, k across 52 sts at back neck. 120 sts. Work in rounds of k2, p2, rib for 2cm/¾in. Cast/bind off in rib.

FINISHING

Set in sleeves. Join side and sleeve seams.

SLEEVE

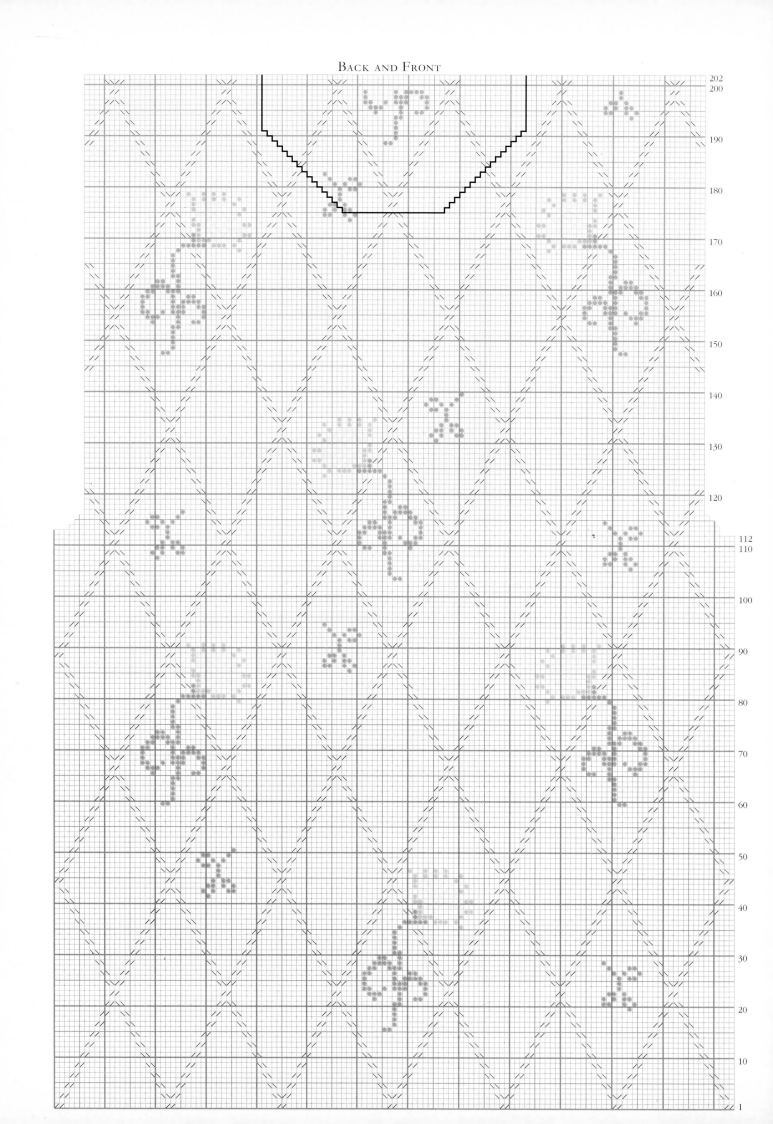

BERLIN

THE FAIR ISLE COLOURWORK FEATURED ON THE YOKE

BRINGS A TOUCH OF TRADITION TO THIS VERY STYLISH TWENTIES-

INSPIRED WOOL CARDIGAN.

◆

MATERIALS
400g/14oz of a 4 ply (US sport weight)
Shetland wool in main colour A
50g/1¾oz each of contrast colours B, C, D, E,
F, G, H and I
Pair each of 2¼mm (US 1), 2¾mm (US 2) and
3¼mm (US 3) knitting needles
7 buttons

MEASUREMENTS
Actual measurements
Bust 97cm/39in
Length to shoulders 63.5cm/25in
Sleeve seam (adjustable) 43cm/17in

TENSION/GAUGE
28 sts and 36 rows to 10cm/4in measured
over st st worked on 3¼mm (US 3) needles

**Please check your tension/gauge carefully
and change needle size if necessary**

BACK
Using 2¾mm (US 2) needles and A cast on
139 sts.
Rib row 1 (RS) K1, * p1, k1, rep from * to
end.
Rib row 2 P1, * k1, p1, rep from * to end.
Rep these 2 rows for 6cm/2½in ending with
rib row 2 and inc 1 st at end of last row.
140 sts.
Change to 3¼mm (US 3) needles and st st.
Dec 1 st at each end of every 7th row until

122 sts rem, now inc 1 st at each end of every
foll 6th row until there are 136 sts.
Cont straight in st st until back measures
39.5cm/15½in from cast-on edge, ending
with a WS row.
Shape armholes
Cast/bind off 3 sts at beg of next 2 rows.
Dec 1 st at each end of the next and 3 foll alt
rows. 122 sts.
Cont straight until back measures 42.5cm/
16¾in from cast-on edge, ending with a RS
row.
Inc row P12, * M1p, p11, rep from * to end.
132 sts.
Work in st st in patt from chart as foll:
Row 1 (RS) Work last 6 sts of row 1, then
work 24 st patt rep 5 times, then work first 6
sts of row 1.
Row 2 Work last 6 sts of row 2, then work 24
st patt rep 5 times, then work first 6 sts of
row 2.
Cont straight in patt as set until back
measures 62cm/24½in from cast-on edge,
ending with a WS row.
Shape neck
Next row Patt 48 sts, turn and leave rem sts
on a spare needle.
Dec 1 st at neck edge of next 4 rows. 44 sts.
Shape shoulder
Cast/bind off.
With right side facing, join yarn to rem sts,
cast/bind off next 36 sts, patt to end.
Dec 1 st at neck edge of next 4 rows. 44 sts.

Shape shoulder
Cast/bind off.

POCKET LININGS (make 2)
Using 3¼mm (US 3) needles and A cast on 34 sts.
Work 21cm/8½in in st st ending with a p row. Leave sts on a spare needle.

LEFT FRONT
Using 2¾mm (US 2) needles and A cast on 65 sts.
Work 6cm/2½in rib as given for back ending with a WS row and increasing 1 st at end of last row. 66 sts.
Change to 3¼mm (US 3) needles and st st.
Dec 1 st at beg of 7th row and at this edge on every foll 7th row until 57 sts rem, now inc 1 st at this edge on every foll 6th row until there are 64 sts **at the same time** when front measures 16.5cm/6½in from cast-on edge ending with a RS row, place pocket as foll.
Place pocket
Next row P 17 sts, place these sts on a holder, with wrong side of pocket to wrong side of front, p next st tog with first st on cast-on edge of pocket, * p next st tog with next st on cast-on edge of pocket, rep from * 32 times more, place rem sts at end of row on a holder, turn.
Change to 2¼mm (US 1) needles and work 2cm/¾in k1, p1 rib on these 34 sts.
Cast/bind off in rib.
Return to sts on left front, p sts on second holder.
Next row K to beg of pocket opening, then k across 34 sts on spare needle of pocket, k across sts on first holder.
Cont in st st, shaping as set, until front measures 39.5cm/15½in from cast-on edge ending at armhole edge.
Shape armhole
Cast/bind off 3 sts at beg of next row.
Dec 1 st at armhole edge of the 4 foll alt rows. 57 sts.
Cont straight until front measures 42.5cm/16¾in from cast-on edge, ending with a RS row.
Inc row P7, * M1p, p10, rep from * to end. 62 sts.
Work in st st in patt from chart as foll:
Row 1 (RS) Work last 6 sts of row 1, then

work 24 st patt rep twice, then work first 8 sts of row 1.
Row 2 Work last 8 sts of row 2, then work 24 st patt rep twice, then work first 6 sts of row 2.
Cont in patt as set until front measures 46cm/18¼in from cast-on edge, ending at neck edge.
Shape neck
Dec 1 st at neck edge of next and every foll 3rd row until 44 sts rem.
Cont straight in patt until front measures the same as back to shoulder shaping ending at armhole edge.

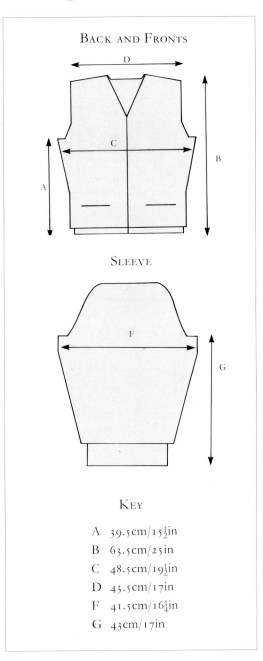

BACK AND FRONTS

SLEEVE

KEY

A 39.5cm/15½in
B 63.5cm/25in
C 48.5cm/19½in
D 43.5cm/17in
F 41.5cm/16¼in
G 43cm/17in

Shape shoulder
Cast/bind off 44 sts.

RIGHT FRONT

Using 2¾mm (US 1) needles and A cast on 65 sts.
Work 6cm/2½in rib as given for back ending with a WS row and increasing 1 st at end of last row. 66 sts.
Change to 3¼mm (US 3) needles and st st.
Dec 1 st at end of 7th row and at this edge on every foll 7th row until 57 sts rem, now inc 1 st at this edge on every foll 6th row until there are 64 sts *at the same time* when front measures 16.5cm/6½in from cast-on edge ending with a RS row, place pocket as foll.

Place pocket

Next row P to last 51 sts, place these sts on a holder, with wrong side of pocket to wrong side of front, p next st tog with first st on cast-on edge of pocket, * p next st tog with next st on cast-on edge of pocket, rep from * 32 times more, place rem sts at end of row on a holder, turn.
Change to 2¼mm (US 1) needles and work 2cm/¾in k1, p1 rib on these 34 sts.
Cast/bind off in rib.
Return to sts on right front, p sts on second holder.

Next row K to beg of pocket opening, then k across 34 sts on spare needle of pocket, k across sts on first holder.
Complete as given for left front reversing all shapings.

SLEEVES

Using 2¼mm (US 1) needles and A cast on 59 sts.

Work 6cm/2½in rib as given for back, ending with a WS row and increasing 1 st at centre of last row. 60 sts.
Change to 3¼mm (US 3) needles and st st.
Inc 1 st at each end of the 3rd and every foll 4th row until there are 116 sts.
Work straight until sleeve measures 43cm/17in from cast-on edge, ending with a WS row.

Shape top
Cast/bind off 3 sts at beg of next 2 rows.
Dec 1 st at each end of the next 5 WS rows. 98 sts.
Work in st st in patt from chart as foll:
Row 1 (RS) Work last 13 sts of row 1, then work 24 st patt rep 3 times, then work first 13 sts of row 1.
Keeping patt correct, dec 1 st at each end of the next and every foll alt row until 84 sts rem, then dec 1 st at each end of the next 31 rows.
Cast/bind off.

FRONT BAND

Using 2¼mm (US 1) needles and A cast on 11 sts.
Rib row 1 K2, [p1, k1] 4 times, k1.
Rib row 2 K1, [p1, k1] 5 times.
Rep these 2 rows until band when slightly stretched fits up left front across back neck and down sloping edge of right front to beg of neck shaping.
Sew band in place.
Sew on buttons to left front, the first to come 1.5cm/½in from lower edge, the seventh level with first row of neck shaping and the remaining five spaced evenly between.
Cont band, working buttonholes to correspond with buttons as follows:
Buttonhole row 1 Rib 4, cast/bind off 3 sts, rib to end.
Buttonhole row 2 Rib 4, cast on 3 sts, rib to end.
Cont in rib, until band reaches cast-on edge of right front.
Cast/bind off.

FINISHING

Set in sleeves. Join side and sleeve seams.
Sew remainder of front band in place. Join sides of pockets to form pocket bags.
Sew row ends of pocket ribs in place.

PATTERN CHART

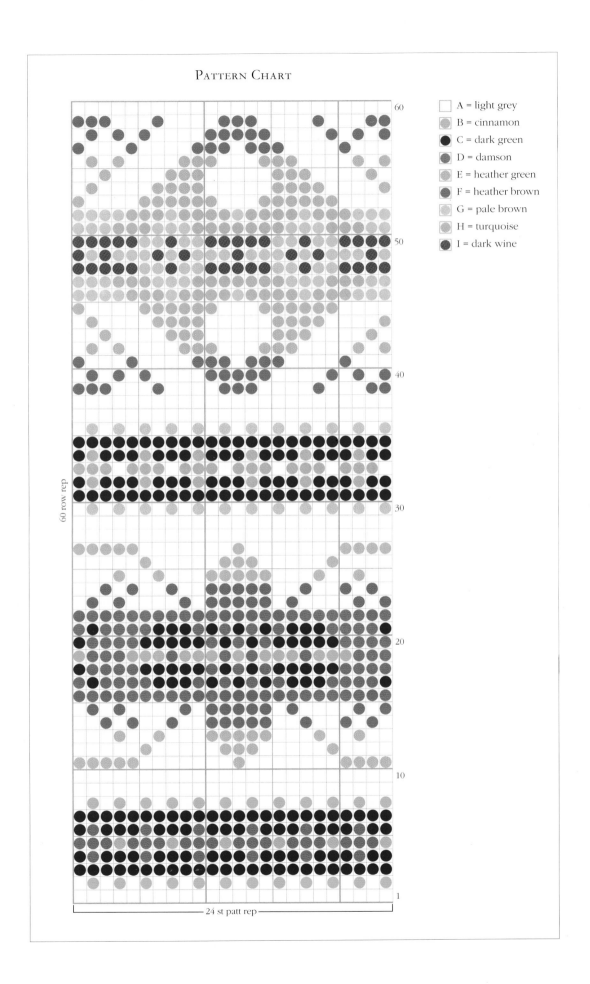

A = light grey
B = cinnamon
C = dark green
D = damson
E = heather green
F = heather brown
G = pale brown
H = turquoise
I = dark wine

60 row rep

24 st patt rep

VENICE

SOMETIMES I FIND IT INTERESTING TO WORK WITHIN THE

CONFINES OF MONOTONE AND TO FIND A HARMONY WITHIN THE

STITCHES WITHOUT THE USE OF COLOUR.

———————◆———————

MATERIALS

Lightweight silk (or cotton—see Note below)

375g/13¼oz for cardigan

150g/5¼oz for top

Pair each of 2¼mm (US 1) and 3mm (US 3) knitting needles

Set of double pointed 2¼mm (US 1) needles

5 buttons for cardigan

MEASUREMENTS

Actual measurements

Cardigan bust 94cm/37in

Cardigan length 65cm/25½in

Cardigan sleeve seams 54cm/21¼in

Top bust 85cm/33in

Top length 53cm/21in

TENSION/GAUGE

30 sts and 40 rows to 10cm/4in measured over patt worked on 3mm (US 3) needles

Please check your tension/gauge carefully and change needle size if necessary

NOTE

These sweaters could also be worked in a light-weight cotton, but would then require approximately double the amount of yarn.

TO MAKE CARDIGAN

BACK

Using smaller needles cast on 102 sts.

Rib row 1 (RS) K2, * p2, k2, rep from * to end.

Rib row 2 P2, * k2, p2, rep from * to end.

Rep these 2 rows for 6cm/2½in ending with rib row 1.

Inc row Rib 2, * M1, rib 3, M1, rib 2, rep from * to end. 142 sts.

Change to larger needles.

Work in patt from chart as follows:

Row 1 (RS) Work last 7 sts of row 1, then work 32 st patt rep 4 times, then work first 7 sts of row 1.

Row 2 Work last 7 sts of row 2, then work 32 st patt rep 4 times, then work first 7 sts of row 2.

Cont straight in patt as set until back measures 42cm/16½in from cast-on edge, ending with a WS row.

Shape armholes

Cast/bind off 8 sts at beg of next 2 rows. 126 sts.

Cont straight in patt until back measures 65cm/25½in from cast-on edge, ending with a WS row.

Shape shoulders

Cast/bind off 19 sts at beg of next 4 rows.

Cast/bind off rem 50 sts.

POCKET LININGS (make 2)

Using larger needles cast on 38 sts.

Beg with a k row, work 13cm/5in in st st ending with a p row.

Leave sts on a spare needle.

LEFT FRONT

Using smaller needles cast on 50 sts.
Work 6cm/2½in rib as given for back ending with a RS row.

Inc row Rib 2, * [M1, rib 2] twice, M1, rib 3, rep from * 5 times more, [M1, rib 2] 3 times. 71 sts.
Change to larger needles.
Work in patt from chart as follows:
Row 1 (RS) Work last 7 sts of row 1, then work 32 st patt rep twice.
Row 2 Work 32 st patt rep twice, then work first 7 sts of row 2.
Cont in patt as set until front measures 19 cm/7½in from cast-on edge ending with a WS row.

Place pocket

Next row Patt 17 sts, slip next 38 sts on to a holder, then patt across 38 sts from one pocket lining, patt rem 16 sts.
Cont in patt until front measures 34cm/13½in from cast-on edge ending with a RS row.

**Shape neck

Dec 1 st at neck edge of next row and 24 foll 4th rows *at the same time* when front measures the same as back to armhole shaping ending at armhole edge shape armhole by casting/binding off 8 sts.
Cont straight in patt until front measures the same as back to shoulder shaping ending at armhole edge.

Shape shoulder

Cast/bind off 19 sts at beg of next row.
Work 1 row.
Cast/bind off rem 19 sts. **

RIGHT FRONT

Using smaller needles cast on 50 sts.
Work 6cm/2½in rib as given for back ending with a RS row.

Inc row Rib 2, * [M1, rib 2] twice, M1, rib 3, rep from * 5 times more, [M1, rib 2] 3 times. 71 sts.
Change to larger needles.
Work in patt from chart as follows:
Row 1 (RS) Work 32 st patt rep of row 1 twice, then work first 7 sts of row 1.
Row 2 Work the last 7 sts of row 2, then work 32 st patt rep twice.
Cont in patt as set until front measures 19cm/7½in from cast-on edge ending with a WS row.

Place pocket

Next row Patt 16 sts, slip next 38 sts on to a holder, then patt across 38 sts from one pocket lining, patt rem 17 sts.
Cont in patt until front measures 34cm/13½in from cast-on edge ending with a RS row.
Complete as given for left front from ** to **.

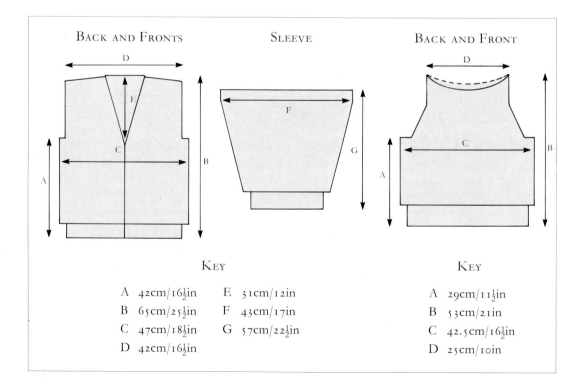

BACK AND FRONTS	SLEEVE	BACK AND FRONT

KEY

		KEY	
A	42cm/16½in	E	31cm/12in
B	65cm/25½in	F	43cm/17in
C	47cm/18½in	G	57cm/22½in
D	42cm/16½in		

KEY

A	29cm/11½in
B	53cm/21in
C	42.5cm/16½in
D	25cm/10in

SLEEVES

Using smaller needles cast on 50 sts.

Work 7.5cm/3in rib as given for back, ending with a RS row.

Inc row Rib 5, * M1, rib 4, M1, rib 5, rep from * to end. 60 sts.

Change to larger needles.

Work in patt from chart as follows:

Row 1 (RS) Work last 14 sts of row 37, then work 32 st patt rep once, then work first 14 sts of row 37.

Row 2 Work last 14 sts of row 38, then work 32 st patt once, then work first 14 sts of row 38.

Keeping patt correct, inc and work into patt 1 st each end of the next and every foll 5th row until there are 130 sts.

Work straight until sleeve measures 57cm/ 22½in from cast-on edge, ending with a WS row.

Cast/bind off.

FRONT BAND

Using smaller needles, cast on 13 sts.

Rib row 1 K2, [p1, k1] 5 times, k1.

Rib row 2 K1, [p1, k1] 6 times.

Rep these 2 rows once more.

*** **Make buttonhole** Rib 7, turn and rib 2 more rows. Break off yarn and rib 3 rows on rem 6 sts, then rib across all sts until rib measures 8cm/3¼in from base of previous buttonhole. ***

Rep from *** to *** 3 times more.

Make a further buttonhole then continue in rib until band when slightly stretched fits up right front, across back neck and down left front.

Cast/bind off.

POCKET TOPS

With right side facing and using smaller needles, k across sts from holder. 38 sts.

Work 7 rows rib as given for back.

Cast/bind off in rib.

FINISHING

Set in sleeves sewing last 8 rows at top of sleeve to sts cast/bound off sts at armhole.

Join side and sleeve seams.

Sew pockets and row ends of pocket ribs in place.

Sew on buttons.

TO MAKE TOP

BACK

Using smaller needles cast on 97 sts.

Rib row 1 (RS) K1, * p1, k1, rep from * to end.

Rib row 2 P1, * k1, p1, rep from * to end.

Rep these 2 rows for 6cm/2½in ending with rib row 1.

Inc row Rib 4, * M1, rib 3, rep from * to end. 128 sts.

Change to larger needles.

Work in patt from pattern chart on page 158 as follows:

Row 1 Work 32 st patt rep of row 1 four times.

Row 2 Work 32 st patt rep of row 2 four times.

Cont straight in patt as set until back measures 29cm/11½in from cast-on edge, ending with a WS row.

PATTERN CHART

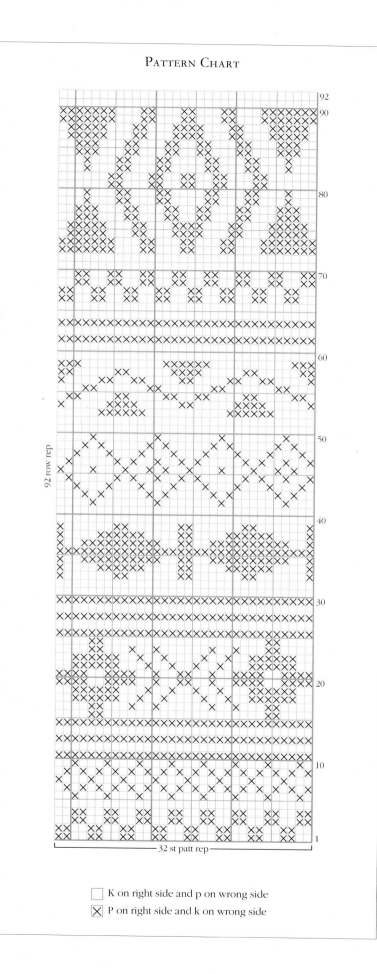

92 row rep

32 st patt rep

☐ K on right side and p on wrong side

☒ P on right side and k on wrong side

Shape armholes
Cast/bind off 8 sts at beg of next 2 rows.
Dec 1 st at each end of the next and every foll alt row until 76 sts rem.
Cont straight in patt until back measures 49 cm/19¼in from cast-on edge, ending with WS row.
Shape neck
Next row Patt 18 sts, turn and leave rem sts on a spare needle.
Dec 1 st at neck edge of next 17 rows.
Fasten off.
With right side facing, return to rem sts and slip next 40 sts on to a spare needle, join on yarn, patt to end.
Dec 1 st at neck edge of next 17 rows.
Fasten off.

FRONT
Work as given for back until front measures 47cm/18½in from beg ending with a WS row.
Shape neck
Next row Patt 25 sts, turn and leave rem sts on a spare needle.
Dec 1 st at neck edge of next 24 rows.
Fasten off.
With right side facing, return to rem sts and slip next 26 sts on to a spare needle, join on yarn, patt to end.
Dec 1 st at neck edge of next 24 rows.
Fasten off.

NECKBAND
Join shoulder points.
Using the set of needles, with right side facing, pick up and k 21 sts down left side of front neck, k across 26 sts from centre front neck, pick up and k 21 sts up right side of front neck, pick up and k 14 sts down right side of back neck, k across 40 sts from centre back neck, pick up and k 14 sts up left side of back neck. 136 sts.
Work in rounds of k1, p1 rib for 1.5cm/½in.
Cast/bind off in rib.

ARMBANDS
Join side seams.
Using the set of needles, with right side facing, pick up and k 160 sts evenly around armhole edge.
Work in rounds of k1, p1 rib for 1.5cm/½in.
Cast/bind off in rib.

KNITTING ABBREVIATIONS

alt — alternate(ly)
approx — approximately
beg — begin(ning)
C4B (cable 4 back) — slip next 2 sts onto a cable needle and leave at back of work, k2, then k2 from cable needle
C4F (cable 4 front) — slip next 2 sts onto a cable needle and leave at front of work, k2, then k2 from cable needle
C6B (cable 6 back) — slip next 3 sts onto a cable needle and leave at back of work, k3, then k3 from cable needle
C6F (cable 6 front) — slip next 3 sts onto a cable needle and leave at front of work, k3, then k3 from cable needle
C8B (cable 8 back) — slip next 4 sts onto a cable needle and leave at back of work, k4, then k4 from cable needle
C8F (cable 8 front) — slip next 4 sts onto a cable needle and leave at front of work, k4, then k4 from cable needle
Cr2R (cross 2 right) — slip next st onto a cable needle and leave at back of work, k1 tbl, k1 from cable needle
Cr2L (cross 2 left) — slip next st onto a cable needle and leave at front of work, k1, k1 tbl from cable needle
Cr2Rp (cross 2 right) — slip next st onto a cable needle and leave at back of work, k1 tbl, p1 from cable needle
Cr2Lp (cross 2 left) — slip next st onto a cable needle and leave at front of work, p1, k1 tbl from cable needle
Cr3R (cross 3 right) — slip next st onto a cable needle and leave at back of work, k2, p1 from cable needle
Cr3L (cross 3 left) — slip next 2 sts onto a cable needle and leave at front of work, p1, k2 from cable needle
Cr4R (cross 4 right) — slip next st onto a cable needle and leave at back of work, k3, p1 from cable needle
Cr4L (cross 4 left) — slip next 3 sts onto a

cable needle and leave at front of work, p1, k3 from cable needle
cont — continu(e)(ing)
dec — decreas(e)(ing)
foll — follow(s)(ing)
g — gramme(s)
g st — garter st
inc — increas(e)(ing)
k — knit
M1 (make one) — * increase one st by inserting left-hand needle from front to back under horizontal strand between last stitch worked and next stitch on left-hand needle, thus forming new st on left-hand needle *, then knit into back of this new st
M1p (make one purlwise) — rep from * to * of M1, then purl into back of this new st
moss st — US seed st
oz — ounce(s)
p — purl
patt — pattern *or* work in pattern (i.e. 'patt 12' means work 12 sts in patt as set)
psso — pass slip stitch over
rem(s) — remain(s)(ing)
rep — repeat(s)(ing)
rev st st — reverse stocking/stockinette stitch
RS — right side(s)
skpo — slip 1, knit 1, psso
sl — slip
st(s) — stitch(es)
st st — stocking/stockinette stitch
tbl — through back of loop(s)
tog — together
Tw2L (twist 2 left) – k into back of second st on left-hand needle, then k first st, slipping both sts off needle together
Tw2R (twist 2 right) — k into front of second st on left hand needle, then k first st, slipping both sts off needle together
WS — wrong side(s)
yo — yarn over right-hand needle to make an extra stitch

CROCHET ABBREVIATIONS

(**Note:** Crochet stitches have different names in the UK and the US. A 'double crochet' in the UK is called a 'single crochet' in the US; and a 'treble' in the UK is called a 'double crochet' in the US. Both terms are given in the instructions. See below.)
ch — chain(s)
dc/sc — double crochet/US single crochet
tr/dc — treble/US double crochet

READING CHARTS

When reading knitting charts, read odd-numbered rows (RS rows) from right to left and even-numbered rows (WS rows) from left to right. All RS rows are k and all WS rows are p, unless indicated otherwise.

KNITTING NEEDLES SIZES

Metric	US	Old UK
2mm	0	14
2¼mm	1	13
2¾mm	2	12
3mm		11
3¼mm	3	10
3½mm	4	
3¾mm	5	9
4mm	6	8
4½mm	7	7
5mm	8	6
5½mm	9	5
6mm	10	4
6½mm	10½	3

ACKNOWLEDGEMENTS

There are many people I would like to thank, not least of all the talented and loyal knitters without whom this book could never have happened. Although there are few of my knitters whom I have met in person, I have talked to many at length on the phone and some have become good friends. Space prevents me mentioning all the knitters but a special big thank you goes to Mrs Shorttle, Mrs Carabine, Mrs Poole, Mrs Banks, Mrs Stammers, Mrs Coe, Mrs Playfor, Mrs Behan, Mrs Hayward-Upton and Mrs Cornish.

I have been very lucky in having a wonderfully professional bunch of people working on my book. Isabel Moore, Linda Burroughs and Peter Butler worked so tirelessly at the beginning of the project. Their enthusiasm and hard work was greatly appreciated. Thanks to everyone else at Paul Hamlyn Publishing. And a special thanks to Bobbie Colgate-Stone for her creative suggestions and meticulous art direction.

Thanks to Penny Hill for editing the patterns. And many thanks to Sally Harding who had the unenviable task of coming in at the eleventh hour to edit the book, but did it with such professionalism and good humour. I don't think anything could faze her!

Tony Boase's beautiful pictures deserve a special mention, as does Jackie

Boase for the endless cups of tea and coffee and delicious food on the shoots. And thanks to Avril Groom who styled the shots.

Thanks to Stephen Sheard and Kathleen Hargreaves at Rowan Yarns for their helpful advice.

Thanks to Bob Tanner, my agent at International Scripts, for his friendship and tireless efforts to get the book off the ground in the early stages.

I cannot end these acknowledgements without saying how much I have appreciated the support and friendship of the many people without whom I could not have written this book during the two years which have been the most difficult in my whole life. To all my family and friends, especially my mother, I extend my love and thanks. A special and warm thanks also to Philip Mercer for his practical help. His suggestions, though not always heeded, were appreciated for the generous and thoughtful way they were given.

Lastly I would like to acknowledge with gratitude the commitment and enthusiasm Brian gave to this project. Although he will never see this book, I feel sure that he would have felt proud to see these designs in print, a goal that he worked so hard towards in our partnership over many years.

Yarn and Kit Information

Buying Yarns

Generic yarn weights are given in the *Materials* section of each knitting pattern in the book. Remember when selecting yarn that the most important factor is matching the gauge required by the pattern. Seek advice at your yarn store if you are unsure about making the correct choice. *Always check your tension/gauge carefully before beginning your garment.*

Rowan Yarns (see addresses below) are suitable for many of the sweaters featured in the book, and we highly recommend these specific yarns for the following sweaters:

Kit Information

The Jean Moss designs followed by an asterisk above are available as kits. To order kits and receive a list of other kits available write to:

Jean Moss Knit Kits, PO Box 1802,
London N4 3EQ, England.

Rowan Yarns Addresses

For details of stockists and mail order sources of Rowan yarns and Rowan kits, please write or contact the following distributors:

United Kingdom: Rowan Yarns, Green Lane Mill, Holmfirth, West Yorkshire, England HD7 1RW. Tel: (0484) 681881

USA: Westminster Trading Corporation, 5 Northern Boulevard, Amherst, NH 03031. Tel: (603) 886 5041

Australia: Sunspun Enterprises Pty Ltd, 191 Canterbury Road, Canterbury 3126, Victoria. Tel: (03) 830 1609

Belgium: Studio Hedera, Deistsestraat 172, B–3030 Leuven. Tel: (016) 232 189

Canada: Estelle Designs and Sales Ltd, Units 65/67, 2220 Midland Avenue, Scarborough, Ontario M1P 3E5. Tel: (416) 298 9922

Denmark: Designer Garn, Aagade 3, Roerbaek, O Hobro. Tel: 9855 7811

Finland: Helmi Vuorelma-Oy, Vesijarven Katu 13, SF–15141 Lahti. Tel: 918 268 31

Germany: Textilwerkstatt, Friedenstrasse 5, 3000 Hanover 1. Tel: 0511 818001

Holland: Henk & Henrietta Beukers, Dorpsstraat 9, 5327 AR Hurwenen. Tel: (04182) 1764

Iceland: Stockurinn, Orlygsdottir, Kjorgardi, Laugavegi 159, 101 Reykjavik. Tel: (91) 182 58

Italy: La Compagnia del Cotone, Via Mazzini 44, 10123 Torino. Tel: (011) 878 381

Japan: Diakeito Co Ltd, 1–5–23 Nakatsu Kita-Ku, Osaka 531. Tel: (06) 371 5657

Mexico: Estambresy Tejidos Finos S.A.DC.V., A.V. Michoacan 30–A, Local 3 Esq Av Mexico, Col Hipodromo Condesa 06170, Mexico 11. Tel: 2 64 84 74

New Zealand: John Q Goldingham Ltd, PO Box 45083, Epuni Railway, Lower Hutt. Tel: (04) 5674 085

Norway: Eureka, PO Box 357, 1401 Ski. Tel: (09) 871 909

Singapore: Classical Hobby House, 1 JLN Anak Bukit, No B2–15 Bukit Timah Plaza, Singapore 2158. Tel: 4662179

Sweden: Wincent, Luntmakargaten 56, 113 58 Stockholm. Tel: (08) 327 060

The publishers would like to thank the following for kindly lending clothes and accessories for photography:-
p 11, Varuna wool skirt, Liberty, London W1; loafers, Russell & Bromley: p 14, silk camisole, Workers for Freedom; earrings, Liberty; wool trousers, MaxMara, London SW1: p 22, cotton bloomers, Spatz, London WC2; hat, The Hat Shop, London W1; jewellery and belt, Santa Fe Trading Post, London W1; quilt, Gallery of Antique Costume and Textiles, London NW1: p 25, sarong skirt, MaxMara; jewellery, Santa Fe Trading Post; p 28, skirt, Maxfield Parrish; shawl and jewellery, Liberty; belt, Santa Fe Trading Post: p 33, Varuna wool skirt, Liberty; hat, The Hat Shop: p 38, silk shirt, Liberty: p 45, cotton shorts, Simpson, London SW1: p 51, antique blouse, Spatz; earrings and bag, Fenwick, London W1: p 54, velvet trousers, Prisma, velvet jacket, Dressage, both at Fenwick: p 59, silk skirt, Workers for Freedom; earrings, Dinny Hall, Fenwick: p 64/65, jeans, Pace; silk scarf, Liberty; belt, Mulberry, London W1: p 70, wool jacket, Marella; wool trousers, Betty Jackson; both at Fenwick; hat, The Hat Shop: p 75, ski pants, Joseph, London SW3; bangle, Liberty: p 78, cotton shirt, Mexx; flannel shorts, Cacharel, both at Liberty; hat, Herbert Johnson, London W1: p 84, trousers, Chinatown, Fenwick: p 90 scarf, Georgina von Etzdorf, London SW1; jodphurs, Freemans catalogue; brooch, Liberty; watch, Fenwick: p 93,

trousers, Marella; shirt, Fenwick; brooch, Butler & Wilson, London W1: p 96/97, trousers, Monsoon; silk top and earrings, Liberty; cap, The Hat Shop; cushions, Pillows, London NW1: p 102, top and earrings, Fenwick; pendant, Dinny Hall; Viyella skirt, Liberty: p 107, scarf, Georgina von Etzdorf; trousers, MaxMara: p 110, blouse, Penny Black, Fenwick; skirt, Cacharel, Liberty; jewellery, Santa Fe Trading Post; hat, The Hat Shop: p 115, blouse, Oui Set, Fenwick; trousers, Joseph; earrings, Liberty; bag, Mulberry: p 118, blouse and skirt, Chinatown; watch, Fenwick: p 125, antique blouse, Rokit, London NW1; trousers, Shaw Cooper; earrings, Fenwick: p 128, skirt and bag, River Island; hat, The Hat Shop; watch, Fior, London SW1: p 132/133, skirt, Prisma, earrings and briefcase, all Fenwick: p 136, skirt and earrings, Fenwick; watch and bracelet, Fior: p 141, antique blouse, Spatz; trousers, I Blues: p 144, skirt, Paddy Campbell, London W1; necklaces, Fior: p 155 & 157, trousers, Mani, Simpson; jewellery, Fior.

The publishers would also like to thank the following organisations for kindly allowing their premises to be used for photography:-
Browns Restaurant and Bar, Cambridge;
Coronation Stables, Newmarket;
Kettle's Yard, Cambridge.